Modern Critical Views

SIGMUND FREUD

Modern Critical Views

SIGMUND FREUD

Edited with an introduction by

Harold Bloom

Sterling Professor of the Humanities
Yale University

1985
CHELSEA HOUSE PUBLISHERS
New York

PROJECT EDITORS: Emily Bestler, James Uebbing
EDITORIAL COORDINATOR: Karyn Browne
EDITORIAL STAFF: Joy Johannessen, Sally Stepanek, Linda Grossman
RESEARCH: Kevin Pask
DESIGN: Susan Lusk

Cover illustration by Peterson Design. Picture courtesy of Culver Pictures
Composition provided by Collage Publications, Inc., New York

Printed and bound in the United States of America

Library of Congress Cataloging in Publication Data
Freud, modern critical views.
    Bibliography: p.
    Includes index.
    Contents: Introduction / Harold Bloom—Eros
and thanatos/Herbert Marcuse—The ethic of
honesty/Philip Rieff—[etc.]
    1. Freud, Sigmund, 1856-1939. 2. Psychoanalysis.
I. Bloom, Harold.
BF173.F85F7415   1984   150.19'52   84-22946
ISBN 0-87754-600-2

Chelsea House Publishers
Harold Steinberg, Chairman & Publisher
Susan Lusk, Vice President
A Division of Chelsea House Educational Communications, Inc.
133 Christopher Street, New York, NY 10014

Contents

Introduction

Sigmund Freud was born on May 6, 1856, and began his characteristic work in Vienna in 1886, when he opened a private practice for the treatment of hysteria. By 1896, before his fortieth birthday, he had begun to use his personal term, "psychoanalysis," to describe what was at once his mode of therapy and his developing theory of the mind. In 1984, nearly a century after Freud began his therapeutic career, it seems incredible that he should have died as much as forty-five years ago, on September 23, 1939, at a still very active eighty-three. We live more than ever in the Age of Freud, despite the relative decline that psychoanalysis has begun to suffer as a public institution and as a medical specialty. Freud's universal and comprehensive theory of the mind probably will outlive the psychoanalytical therapy, and seems already to have placed him with Plato and Montaigne and Shakespeare rather than with the scientists he overtly aspired to emulate.

This is not to suggest that Freud was primarily a philosopher, an essayist or a poet, but rather that his influence has been analogous to that of Plato, Montaigne, Shakespeare: inescapable, immense, almost incalculable. In some sense, we are all Freudians, whether we want to be or not. Freud is much more than a perpetual fashion: he seems to have become a culture, our culture. He is at once the principal writer and the principal thinker of our century. If one seeks the strongest authors in the West in our time, most readers would agree upon the crucial figures; Proust, Joyce, Kafka, Yeats, Mann, Lawrence, Eliot, Rilke, Faulkner, Valéry, Stevens, Montale, Beckett certainly would be among them. The essential thinkers might constitute a shorter and more controversial canon, whether of scientists or philosophers, and I will not venture to list them here. Freud is unique in that he would dominate the second group and successfully challenge even Proust, Joyce, Kafka in the first. Nor can one match him with any of the religious figures or scholars of the century. His only rivals indeed are Plato, Montaigne, Shakespeare, or even the anonymous primal narrator of Genesis, Exodus and Numbers, called the "J" writer or Yahwist in biblical scholarship.

It is this unique stature, this pervasive influence of Freud, that now constitutes the overwhelming element in his achievement. Perhaps his effect upon us is even more important than the apparently lasting value of his general theory of the mind. Himself the creator of the darkest Western vision of fatherhood since the ancient Gnostics, he has become a generic father figure in Western culture, a fate he would have resented. His Viennese contemporary, the satirist Karl Kraus, bitterly observed that psychoanalysis itself was the mental illness or spiritual disease of which it purported to be the cure. This remains, I think, the most destructive remark that Freud ever has provoked, because it centers upon what is most problematic in his writing and in his therapy, the intimately related ideas of authority and transference.

In the name of *his* science, Freud audaciously usurped authority and triumphantly manifested an originality comparable even to Shakespeare's. Perhaps he subsumed Schopenhauer and Nietzsche in something of the way in which Shakespeare can be said to have swallowed up Christopher Marlowe. Iago and Edmund have traces of the Marlovian hero-villain, but *Othello* and *Lear* are universes of language, while *The Jew of Malta* and *Tamburlaine* in comparison seem only local regions of powerful rhetoric. Schopenhauer lurks uneasily in the Freudian mythology of the drives, and Nietzsche's tracing of the genealogy of morals perhaps haunts Freud's account of our need for punishment, the economics of moral masochism. But we read Marlowe now in the shadow of Shakespeare, and the psychoanalytical acuity of Nietzsche and Schopenhauer appears fitful in direct juxtaposition to Freud's uncanny stories of our unconscious mental processes. "Great havoc makes he among our originalities," Emerson ruefully observed of Plato, and Emerson came near to saying the same of Montaigne and of Shakespeare. We must say of Freud: after him there is only commentary.

II

To begin is to be free, and after Freud we are never free of Freud. His peculiar subject was psychic overdetermination or unconscious bondage, or again, the inability to begin freshly rather than to repeat. Eros, he taught, is never free but always a repetition, always a transference in authority from past to present. Presumably just this sense of enforced illusion gave Freud his double concept of taboo and transference, two heightened versions of emotional ambivalence, of simultaneous love and hatred invested in the same object to a nearly equal degree, a conflict manifested in that other masterpiece of emotional ambivalence, the Oedipal complex. Love, reliant upon the fixations of infantile sexuality for its origins, suffers always from the felt stigma of the narcissistic scar, the infant's first tragic failure in sexual strife or its loss of the parent of the opposite sex to the rival, the parent of the same sex. Already necessarily neurotic, love thus is usefully vulnerable to the "artificial neuroses" of the psychoanalytic transference, the false Eros induced by Freud and his followers for therapeutic purposes, or as a fresh wound inflicted supposedly to heal a wound.

The analytical transference marks the crisis in Freud's vision of Eros, a crisis that is the hidden point of Karl Kraus's bitter jest that psychoanalysis itself was the mental disease for which it pretended to be the cure. By 1984, psychoanalysis in a societal sense has become a kind of universal transference neurosis, and the figure of Freud has assumed a mythological status darkly akin to that of the totemic father who is slain and devoured in the ghastly Primal History Scene of *Totem and Taboo*. As the dead father, Freud is stronger than any living father can be, indeed has blended into the man Moses, a new Moses, to be sure, replacing monotheism, but hardly with the religion of science. The dead ancestor has become a numinous shadow for his adherents, by a Nietzschean irony that haunts many other modern secularisms.

III

The late Michel Foucault once observed that Marxism swims in nineteenth-century thought as a fish swims in the sea. One could not make the same remark about what I suggest we begin to call the Freudian speculation. Though Freud emerged from the Age of Darwin, he is a curiously timeless figure, as old as Jewish memory. His Jewishness is far more central to him than he cared to believe and, together with Kafka's, may be retrospectively definitive of what Jewish culture can still be as the end of this century approaches. Gershom Scholem, who loved Kafka's writings and rather resented Freud's, said of Kafka's that they had for certain readers (like Scholem) "something of the strong light of the canonical, of that perfection which destroys." For certain other readers (like myself, and like the other contributors to this volume) Freud's writings share that quality with Kafka's. Though barely touched by normative Judaism, Freud and Kafka were Jewish writers, just as Scholem was. Someday, perhaps, all three together will be seen as having redefined Jewish culture among them.

Freud, in his overt polemic against religion, insisted upon reducing all religion to the longing for the father. This reduction makes sense only in an Hebraic universe of discourse, where authority always resides in figures of the individual's past and only rarely survives in the individual proper. The Greek spirit encouraged an individual agon for contemporary authority, an agon made possible by the example of the Homeric heroes. But if the hero is Abraham or Jacob rather than Achilles or Odysseus, he provides a much more anxious example. Plato was ironically Homeric in entering upon a struggle with Homer for the mind of Athens, but the Rabbi Akiba would never have seen himself as struggling with Moses for the mind of Jerusalem. Zeus was not incommensurate with the godlike Achilles. Abraham, arguing with Yahweh on the road to Sodom, haggled with God over the number of righteous men required to prevent the destruction of the city but knew he was nothing in himself when face to face with Yahweh. Yet in his humane desperation, Father Abraham pragmatically needed to act momentarily as if he were everything in himself. It is Jewish, and not Greek, to vacillate so dizzily between the need to be everything in oneself and the anxiety of being nothing in oneself. That vertigo is the condition that makes necessary what Freud called defense or repression, the flight from prohibited representations of desire.

But what are the motives for such flight, for the defense or repression? Since Freud defines the drive as that which yields pleasure when fulfilled, what is it that sets off, by displeasure, repression? I find no overt answer to this crucial question in Freud, whose characteristic dualism was too fundamental for questioning. The only answer is implicit in the dualism, a point shrewdly noted by the Dutch historical psychologist J. H. Van den Berg: "The theory of repression . . . is closely related to the thesis that there is sense in everything, which in turn implies that everything is past and there is nothing new." That is to say, we can understand repression only in a psychic world where everything is absolutely meaningful, where a symptom or a witticism or a verbal slip is so overdetermined that enormous interpretative intensity can and must be applied. Such a world, the realm of the great normative rabbis and of Freud, ensues when everything is over already, when the truly significant has happened once and for all. The time of the fathers, for the rabbis, is akin to Freud's age of infancy, when we are scarred forever.

What for the rabbis was significant memory appears in Freud, under the sign of negation, as unconscious but purposeful forgetting, or repression. But this Freudian negation is precisely Jewish or rabbinical, marked by the Hebraic mode of dualism, which is not a split between mind or soul and body, or between the self and nature, but a subtler dichotomy between inwardness and outwardness. This is prophetic dualism, the stance of Elijah and of the line of his successors from Amos to Malachi. In standing against the unjust world, Elijah and his disciples proclaim that justice must be established *against the world*, in a deep inwardness of morality that wars against all outwardness whatsoever. But what is this, in the Freudian register, except the moral basis for Freud's only transcendence, which is reality testing, or learning to live with the reality principle? Why, after all, is the psyche at civil war? What does it war with, in itself, except the injustice of outwardness, the repressive vicissitudes of the drives, the neurotic sufferings that rob us of the freedom that yet can give time to time, so that for a moment it might be our time?

IV

To mistake Freudian negation is to destroy his dualisms, a destruction of more than just his intrinsic Jewishness, and yet this is precisely the ironic effect of what has come to be called "French Freud," the revisionary reading of Freud carried through by the late Jacques Lacan and his followers. Essentially, this has involved the Hegelianizing of Freud, a harmless enough enterprise but rather odd, since the Freudian speculation rarely evades for very long the ultimate authority of given fact. Herbert Marcuse, who did not confuse Freud with Hegel, analyzed Hegel's intellectual optimism as being based upon a destructive concept of the given, with knowledge originating when philosophy destroyed the experience of daily life, by way of a double process of negation, first being the negation of every object, and second the negation of the individual ego. That, as Marcuse knew, is not Freud, but it is the antiempirical Freud of Lacan, Laplanche and Derrida. French Freud features the reduction of the actual Freud's metapsychological dualism to a mere psychical duplicity, fit expression of a psycholinguistic skepticism. The effect of this reduction is to undo Freud's more radical dualisms, between primary and secondary processes, and between the pleasure and reality principles. But the final consequence is that the Freudian theory of the mind is converted into a kind of phantasmagoric monism, in which the primal ambivalence of monistic narcissism becomes our ruling passion. The psyche's civil war will then take place *within* a narcissistic, mostly unconscious ego, rather than between ego and id, or ego and superego. Freud would cease to be a dualist, and the irony of Lacan's accomplishment will have been to revise Freud into a monism as flat as Alfred Adler's.

Doubtless, an adherent of French Freud could respond that whatever distortion Lacan or Derrida brings about is still preferable to the revisionary ego psychology of Heinz Hartmann or the severe modifications made by the British followers of Melanie Klein. Our inability to characterize Freud accurately without revising him is a true sign of his varied strength. His central ideas—the drives, the defenses, the psychic agencies, the dynamic unconscious—are all frontier concepts, making ghostlier the demarcations between mind and body. Freud's science, psychoanalysis, is neither primarily speculative/poetic nor empirical/therapeutic but is on the border between all prior disciplines. So his concept of negation is a frontier idea also, breaking down the distinction between inwardness and outwardness. In Freudian negation, as in normative Jewish memory, a previously repressed thought, desire or feeling achieves formulation only by being disowned, so that it is cognitively accepted but still affectively denied. Thinking is freed from its sexual past, even as thinking is desexualized also in the rituals of normative Judaism.

Richard Wollheim brilliantly relates Freud's idea of negation to Freud's difficult realization that the ego is always a bodily ego. So, the capacity to assign truth or falsehood to an assertion is traced to a primitive movement of mind, wherein a kind of thought is felt and is then either introjected (swallowed up) or projected (spat out). This explains how negation works so as to internalize certain objects of the mind, an internalization that results in the bodily ego. But both an "internalized object" and a "bodily ego" are very difficult fictions or metaphors. How after all can a thought become an object, even if that object has been introjected by one's bodily ego? Freud's language here is radically poetic and mythological, akin to the prophetic language of an intensified moral inwardness that itself personifies justice, and that also broke down the frontiers between the soul and the outward world.

V

The essays and excerpts gathered in this volume are by four philosophers (two French, one British, one German), three psychiatrists (two French, one Dutch), two American literary critics and one American sociologist. Nothing unites them, beyond their intense concern with Freud. They are reprinted in the order of their publication, and they record the phases in which Freud's speculative and imaginative challenge has been felt though hardly answered. I conclude this introduction by returning to Emerson on Plato in *Representative Men*, because what Emerson says of Plato there seems to me true of Freud also:

> There was never such range of speculation. Out of Plato come all things that are still written and debated among men of thought. Great havoc makes he among our originalities. We have reached the mountain from which all these drift boulders were detached. . . .

HERBERT MARCUSE

Eros and Thanatos

Under non-repressive conditions, sexuality tends to "grow into" Eros—that is to say, toward self-sublimation in lasting and expanding relations (including work relations) which serve to intensify and enlarge instinctual gratification. Eros strives for "eternalizing" itself in a permanent *order*. This striving finds its first resistance in the realm of necessity. To be sure, the scarcity and poverty prevalent in the world could be sufficiently mastered to permit the ascendancy of universal freedom, but this mastery seems to be self-propelling—perpetual labor. All the technological progress, the conquest of nature, the rationalization of man and society have not eliminated and cannot eliminate the necessity of alienated labor, the necessity of working mechanically, unpleasurably, in a manner that does not represent individual self-realization.

However, progressive alienation itself increases the potential of freedom: the more external to the individual the necessary labor becomes, the less does it involve him in the realm of necessity. Relieved from the requirements of domination, the quantitative reduction in labor time and energy leads to a qualitative change in the human existence: the free rather than the labor time determines its content. The expanding realm of freedom becomes truly a realm of play—of the free play of individual faculties. Thus liberated, they will generate new forms of realization and of discovering the world, which in turn will reshape the realm of necessity, the struggle for existence. The altered relation between the two realms of the human reality alters the relation between what is desirable and what is reasonable, between instinct and reason. With the transformation from sexuality into Eros, the life instincts evolve their sensuous order, while reason becomes sensuous to the degree to which it comprehends and organizes necessity in terms of protecting instincts evolve their sensuous order, while reason becomes sensuous to the degree to which it comprehends and organizes necessity in terms of protecting and enriching the life instincts. The roots of the aesthetic experience re-emerge—not merely in an artistic culture but in the struggle for existence itself. It assumes a new rationality. The repressiveness of reason that characterizes the rule of the performance principle does not belong to the realm of necessity *per se*. Under the performance principle, the gratification of the sex instinct depends largely on the "suspension" of reason and even of consciousness: on the brief (legitimate or furtive) oblivion of the private and the universal unhappiness, on the interruption of the reasonable routine of life, of the duty and dignity of status and office. Happiness is almost by definition unreasonable if it is unrepressed and uncontrolled. In contrast, beyond the performance principle, the gratification of the instinct requires the more conscious effort of free rationality, the less it is the by-product of the superimposed rationality of oppression. The more freely the instinct develops, the more freely will its "conservative nature" assert itself. The striving for *lasting* gratification makes not only for an enlarged order of libidinal relations ("community") but also for the perpetuation of this order on a higher scale. The pleasure principle extends to consciousness. Eros redefines reason in his own terms. Reasonable is what sustains the order of gratification.

To the degree to which the struggle for existence becomes co-operation for the free development and fulfillment of individual needs, repressive reason gives way to a new *rationality of gratification* in which reason and happiness converge. It creates its own division of labor, its own priorities, its own hierarchy. The historical heritage of the performance principle is administration, not of men, but of things: mature civilization depends for its functioning on a multitude of co-ordinated arrangements. These arrangements in turn must carry recognized and recognizable authority. Hierarchical relationships are not unfree *per se*; civilization relies to a great extent on rational authority, based on knowledge and necessity, and aiming at the protection and preservation of life. Such is the authority of the engineer, of the traffic policeman, of the airplane pilot in flight. Once again, the distinction between repression and surplus-repression must be recalled. If a child feels the "need" to cross the street any time at its will, repression of this "need" is not repressive of human potentialities. It may be the opposite. The need to "relax" in the entertainments furnished by the culture industry is itself repressive, and its repression is a step toward freedom. Where repression has become so effective that, for the repressed, it assumes the (illusory) form of freedom, the abolition of such freedom readily appears as a totalitarian act. Here, the old conflict arises again: human freedom is not only a private affair—but it is nothing at all unless it is *also* a private affair. Once privacy must no longer be maintained apart from and against the public existence, the liberty of the individual and that of the whole may perhaps be reconciled by a "general will" taking shape in institutions which are directed toward the individual needs. The renunciations and delays demanded by the general will must not be opaque and inhuman; nor must their reason be authoritarian. However, the question remains: how can civilization freely generate freedom, when unfreedom has become part and parcel of the mental apparatus? And if not, who is entitled to establish and enforce the objective standards?

From Plato to Rousseau, the only honest answer is the idea of an educational dictatorship, exercised by those who are supposed to have acquired knowledge of the real Good. The answer has since become obsolete: knowledge of the available means for creating a humane existence for all is no longer confined to a privileged elite. The facts are all too open, and the individual consciousness would safely arrive at them if it were not methodically arrested and diverted. The distinction between rational and irrational authority, between repression and surplus-repression, can be made and verified by the individuals themselves. That they cannot make this distinction now does not mean that they cannot learn to make it once they are given the opportunity to do so. Then the course of trial and error becomes a rational course in freedom. Utopias are susceptible to unrealistic blueprints; the conditions for a free society are not. They are a matter of reason.

It is not the conflict between instinct and reason that provides the strongest argument against the idea of a free civilization, but rather the conflict which instinct creates in itself. Even if the destructive forms of its polymorphous perversity and license are due to surplus-repression and become susceptible to libidinal order once surplus-repression is removed, instinct itself is beyond good and evil, and no free civilization can dispense with this distinction. The mere fact that, in the choice of its objects, the sex instinct is not guided by reciprocity constitutes a source of unavoidable conflict among individuals—and a strong argument against the possibility of its self-sublimation. But is there perhaps in the instinct itself an inner barrier which "contains" its driving power? Is there perhaps a "natural" self-restraint in Eros so that its genuine gratification would call for delay, detour, and arrest? Then there would be obstructions and limitations imposed not from outside, by a repressive reality principle, but set and accepted by the instinct itself because they have inherent libidinal value. Freud indeed suggested this notion. He thought that "unrestrained sexual liberty from the beginning" results in lack of full satisfaction:

> It is easy to show that the value the mind sets on erotic need instantly sinks as soon as satisfaction becomes readily obtainable. Some obstacle is necessary to swell the tide of the libido to its height.

Moreover, he considered the "strange" possibility that "something in the nature of the sexual instinct is unfavorable to the achievement of absolute gratification." The idea is ambiguous and lends itself easily to ideological justifications: the unfavorable consequences of readily available satisfaction have probably been one of the strongest props for repressive morality. Still, in the context of Freud's theory, it would follow that the "natural obstacles" in the instinct, far from denying pleasure, may function as a premium on pleasure if they are divorced from archaic taboos and exogenous constraints. Pleasure contains an element of self-determination which is the token of human triumph over blind necessity:

> Nature does not know real pleasure but only satisfaction of want. All pleasure is societal—in the unsublimated no less than in the sublimated impulses. Pleasure originates in alienation.

What distinguishes pleasure from the blind satisfaction of want is the instinct's refusal to exhaust itself in immediate satisfaction, its ability to build up and use barriers for intensifying fulfillment. Though this instinctual refusal has done the work of domination, it can also serve the opposite function: eroticize non-libidinal relations, transform biological tension and relief into free happiness. No longer employed as instruments for retaining men in alienated performances, the barriers against absolute gratification would become elements of human freedom; they would protect that other alienation in which pleasure originates—man's alienation not from himself but from mere nature: his free self-realization. Men would really exist as individuals, each shaping his own life; they would face each other with truly different needs and truly different modes of satisfaction—with their own refusals and their own selections. The ascendancy of the pleasure principle would thus engender antagonisms, pains, and frustrations—individual conflicts in the striving for gratification. But these conflicts would themselves have libidinal value: they would be permeated with the rationality of gratification. This *sensuous* rationality contains its own moral laws.

The idea of a libidinal morality is suggested not only by Freud's notion of instinctual barriers to absolute gratification, but also by psychoanalytic interpretations of the superego. It has been pointed out that the superego, as the mental representative of morality, is not unambiguously the representative of the reality principle, especially of the forbidding and punishing father. In many cases, the superego seems to be in secret alliance with the id, defending the claims of the id against the ego and the external world. Charles Odier therefore proposed that a part of the superego is "in the last analysis the representative of a primitive phase, during which morality had not yet freed itself from the pleasure principle." He speaks of a pregenital, prehistoric, preoedipal "pseudo-morality" prior to the acceptance of the reality principle, and calls the mental representative of this "pseudo-morality" the *superid*. The psychical phenomenon which, in the individual, suggests such a pregenital morality is an identification with the mother, expressing itself in a castration-wish rather than castration-threat. It might be the survival of a regressive tendency: remembrance of the primal Mother-Right, and at the same time a "symbolic means against losing the then prevailing privileges of the woman." According to Odier, the pregenital and prehistorical morality of the superid is incompatible with the reality principle and therefore a neurotic factor.

One more step in the interpretation, and the strange traces of the "superid" appear as traces of a different, lost reality, or lost relation between ego and reality. The notion of reality which is predominant in Freud and which is condensed in the reality principle is "bound up with the father." It confronts the id and the ego as a hostile, external force, and, accordingly, the father is chiefly a hostile figure, whose power is symbolized in the castration-threat, "directed against the gratification of libidinal urges toward the mother." The growing ego attains maturity by complying with this hostile force: "submission to the castration threat" is the "decisive step in the establishment of the ego as based on the reality principle." However, this reality which the ego faces as an outside antagonistic power is neither the only nor the primary reality. The development of the ego is development "away from primary narcissism"; at this early stage, reality "is not outside, but is contained in the pre-ego of primary narcissism." It is not hostile and alien to the ego, but "intimately connected with, originally not even distinguished from it." This reality is first (and last?) experienced in the child's libidinal relation to the mother—a relation which is at the beginning within the "pre-ego" and only subsequently divorced from it. And with this division of the original unity, an "urge towards re-establishing the original unity" develops: a "libidinal flow between infant and mother." At this primary stage of the relation between "pre-ego" and reality, the Narcissistic and the maternal Eros seem to be one, and the primary experience of reality is that of a libidinous union. The Narcissistic phase of individual pre-genitality "recalls" the maternal phase of the history of the human race. Both constitute a reality to which the ego responds with an attitude, not of defense and submission, but of integral identification with the "environment." But in the light of the paternal reality principle, the "maternal concept" of reality here emerging is immediately turned into something negative, dreadful. The impulse to re-establish the lost Narcissistic-maternal unity is interpreted as a "threat," namely, the threat of "maternal engulfment" by the overpowering womb. The hostile father is exonerated and reappears as savior who, in punishing the incest wish, protects the ego from its annihilation in the mother. The question does not arise whether the Narcissistic-maternal attitude toward reality cannot "return" in less primordial, less devouring forms under the power of the mature ego and in a mature civilization. Instead, the necessity of suppressing this attitude once and for all is taken for granted. The patriarchal reality principle holds sway over the psychoanalytic interpretation. It is only beyond this reality principle that the "maternal" images of the superego convey promises rather than memory traces—images of a free future rather than of a dark past.

However, even if a maternal libidinal morality is traceable in the instinctual structure, and even if a sensuous rationality could make the Eros freely susceptible to order, one innermost obstacle seems to defy all project of a non-repressive development—namely, the bond that binds Eros to the death instinct. The brute fact of death denies once and for all the reality of a non-repressive existence. For death is the final negativity of time, but "joy wants eternity." Timelessness is the ideal of pleasure. Time has no power over the id, the original domain of the pleasure principle. But the ego, through which alone pleasure becomes real, is in its entirety subject to time. The mere anticipation of the inevitable end, present in every instant, introduces a repressive element into all libidinal relations and renders pleasure itself painful. This primary frustration in the instinctual structure of man becomes the inexhaustible source of all other frustrations—and of their social effectiveness. Man learns that "it cannot last anyway," that every pleasure is short, that for all finite things the hour of their birth is the hour of their death—that it couldn't be otherwise. He is resigned before society forces him to practice resignation methodically. The flux of time is society's most natural ally in maintaining law and order, conformity, and the institutions that relegate freedom to a perpetual utopia; the flux of time helps men to forget what was and what can be: it makes them oblivious to the better past and the better future.

This ability to forget—itself the result of a long and terrible education by experience—is an indispensable requirement of mental and physical hygiene without which civilized life would be unbearable; but it is also the mental faculty which sustains submissiveness and renunciation. To forget is also to forgive what should not be forgiven if justice and freedom are to prevail. Such forgiveness reproduces the conditions which reproduce injustice and enslavement: to forget past suffering is to forgive the forces that caused it—without defeating those forces. The wounds that heal in time are also the wounds that contain the poison. Against this surrender to time, the restoration of remembrance to its rights, as a vehicle of liberation, is one of the noblest tasks of thought. In this function, remembrance (*Erinnerung*) appears at the conclusion of Hegel's *Phenomenology of the Spirit*; in this function, it appears in Freud's theory. Like the ability to forget, the ability to remember is a product of civilization—perhaps its oldest and most fundamental psychological achievement. Nietzsche saw in the training of memory the beginning of civilized morality—especially the memory of obligations, contracts, dues. This context reveals the one-sidedness of memory-training in civilization: the faculty was chiefly directed toward remembering duties rather than pleasures; memory was linked with bad conscience, guilt, and sin. Unhappiness and the threat of punishment, not happiness and the promise of freedom, linger in memory.

Without release of the repressed content of memory, without release of its liberating power, non-repressive sublimation is unimaginable. From the myth of Orpheus to the novel of Proust, happiness and freedom have been linked with the idea of the recapture of time: the *temps retrouvé*. Remembrance retrieves the *temps perdu*, which was the time of gratification and fulfillment. Eros, penetrating into consciousness, is moved by remembrance; with it he protests against the order of renunciation; he uses memory in his effort to defeat time in a world dominated by time. But in so far as time retains its power over Eros, happiness is essentially a thing of the *past*. The terrible sentence which states that only the lost paradises are the true ones judges and at the same time rescues the *temps perdu*. The lost paradises are the only true ones not because, in retrospect, the past joy seems more beautiful than it really was, but because remembrance alone provides the joy without the anxiety over its passing and thus gives it an otherwise impossible duration. Time loses its power when remembrance redeems the past.

Still, this defeat of time is artistic and spurious; remembrance is no real weapon unless it is translated into historical action. Then, the struggle against time becomes a decisive movement in the struggle against domination:

> The conscious wish to break the continuum of history belongs to the revolutionary classes in the moment of action. This consciousness asserted itself during the July Revolution. In the evening of the first day of the struggle, simultaneously but independently at several places, shots were fired at the time pieces on the towers of Paris.

It is the alliance between time and the order of repression that motivates the efforts to halt the flux of time, and it is this alliance that makes time the deadly enemy of Eros. To be sure, the threat of time, the passing of the moment of fullness, the anxiety over the end, may themselves become erotogenic—obstacles that "swell the tide of the libido." However, the wish of Faust which conjures the pleasure principle demands, not the beautiful moment, but eternity. With its striving for eternity, Eros offends against the decisive taboo that sanctions libidinal pleasure only as a temporal and controlled condition, not as a permanent fountainhead of the human existence. Indeed, if the alliance between time and the established order dissolved, "natural" private unhappiness would no longer support organized societal unhappiness. The relegation of human fulfillment to utopia would no longer find adequate response in the instincts of man, and the drive for liberation would assume that terrifying force which actually it never had. Every sound reason is on the side of law and order in their insistence that the eternity of joy be reserved for the hereafter, and in their endeavor to subordinate the struggle against death and disease to the never-ceasing requirements of national and international security.

The striving for the preservation of time in time, for the arrest of time, for conquest of death, seems unreasonable by any standard, and outright impossible under the hypothesis of the death instinct that we have accepted. Or does this very hypothesis make it more reasonable? The death instinct operates under the Nirvana principle: it tends toward that state of "constant gratification" where no tension is felt—a state without want. This trend of the instinct implies that its *destructive* manifestations would be minimized as it approached such a state. If the instinct's basic objective is not the termination of life but of pain—the absence of tension—then paradoxically, in terms of the instinct, the conflict between life and death is the more reduced, the closer life approximates the state of gratification. Pleasure principle and Nirvana principle then converge. At the same time, Eros, freed from surplus-repression, would be strengthened, and the strengthened Eros would, as it were, absorb the objective of the death instinct. The instinctual value of death would have changed: if the instincts pursued and attained their fulfillment in a nonrepressive order, the regression compulsion would lose much of its biological rationale. As suffering and want recede, the Nirvana principle may become reconciled with the reality principle. The unconscious attraction that draws the instincts back to an "earlier state" would be effectively counteracted by the desirability of the attained state of life. The "conservative nature" of the instincts would come to rest in a fulfilled present. Death would cease to be an instinctual goal. It remains a fact, perhaps even an ultimate necessity—but a necessity against which the unrepressed energy of mankind will protest, against which it will wage its greatest struggle.

In this struggle, reason and instinct could unite. Under conditions of a truly human existence, the difference between succumbing to disease at the age of ten, thirty, fifty, or seventy, and dying a "natural" death after a fulfilled life, may well be a difference worth fighting for with all instinctual energy. Not those who die, but those who die before they must and want to die, those who die in agony and pain, are the great indictment against civilization. They also testify to the unredeemable guilt of mankind. Their death arouses the painful awareness that it was unnecessary, that it could be otherwise. It takes all the institutions and values of a repressive order to pacify the bad conscience of this guilt. Once again, the deep connection between the death instinct and the sense of guilt becomes apparent. The silent "professional agreement" with the fact of death and disease is perhaps one of the most widespread expressions of the death instinct—or, rather, of its social usefulness. In a repressive civilization, death itself becomes an instrument of repression. Whether death is feared as constant threat, or glorified as supreme sacrifice, or accepted as fate, the education for consent to death introduces an element of surrender into life from the beginning—surrender and submission. It stifles "utopian" efforts. The powers that be have a deep affinity to death; death is a token of unfreedom, of defeat. Theology and philosophy today compete with each other in celebrating death as an existential category: perverting a biological fact into an ontological essence, they bestow transcendental blessing on the guilt of mankind which they help to perpetuate—they betray the promise of utopia. In contrast, a philosophy that does not work as the handmaiden of repression responds to the fact of death with the Great Refusal—the refusal of Orpheus the liberator. Death can become a token of freedom. The necessity of death does not refute the possibility of final liberation. Like the other necessities, it can be made rational—painless. Men can die without anxiety if they know that what they love is protected from misery and oblivion. After a fulfilled life, they may take it upon themselves to die—at a moment of their own choosing. But even the ultimate advent of freedom cannot redeem those who died in pain. It is the remembrance of them, and the accumulated guilt of mankind against its victims, that darken the prospect of a civilization without repression.

PHILIP RIEFF

The Ethic of Honesty

Honesty, granting that it is the virtue from which we cannot rid ourselves, we free spirits — well, we will labor at it with all our perversity and love, and not tire of "perfecting" ourselves in our virtue, which alone remains. . . .

—NIETZSCHE

From the beginning, Freud enunciated his science as a therapy. The significance of this is immense: bereft of religion and betrayed by the spurious objectivity of so many sciences, the modern mind has found nothing so convincing as a science that is at the same time a casuistry of the intimate and everyday life. Freudianism restored to science its ethical verve. That it did so by putting ethics itself under the scrutiny of science, as part of the therapeutic purpose of the science, is all the more reason for its appeal. In this way Freud has given us a popular science of morals that also teaches a moral system.

Belief cannot be separated from theory, any more than theory is separable from its consequences. As the rationalized mythology of our culture, modern science has played a larger role in reformulating our moral sense that its defenders often care to admit. Scientific theories function as new and powerful modes of personal belief. Psychoanalysis cannot disclaim its influence on the day-to-day consciousness of our age by calling itself simply a science. All the issues which psychoanalysis treats—the health and sickness of the will, the emotions, the responsibilities of private living, the coercions of culture—belong to the moral life. As a pathologist of the moral sense, Freud could in fact capitalize on the authority gained by science as a cultural ideal. Science claims simply to work. It frees man to observe, to present the facts honestly and come to no conclusion—while at the same time it passes the most detailed judgments and patently takes moral effect. Freud's reticence as a moralist has made him the more influential. His moralizing is of the sort peculiar to our age, most effective when executed with a bad conscience. He set himself up as the amateur moralist, not in the pay of any system, a strict scientist in search of hard facts who, in passing, could not avoid throwing light on the dark corners out of which morality grows.

I

While sometimes claiming that analysis was "entirely non-tendentious," Freud elsewhere recognized that his science was as much philosophy as medicine. Psychoanalysis stands, he said, in a "middle position between medicine and philosophy." Freud was anxious that analysis make the best of both worlds. He himself had "never really been a doctor in the proper sense." With a fine mordant flourish, he boasted that he lacked "a genuine medical temperament," the "innate sadistic disposition." As a child, he had never liked to "play the 'doctor game.'" His "original objective" was philosophy; the shift from neurology to psychology satisfied his longing for philosophical knowledge; "psychology was just a way of expressing this." More interested in problems than in patients, he had become a doctor against his will. But, having made himself over into a new kind of doctor, Freud could claim all society as his patient. It is the ambition of his claim that separates Freud and the psychoanalysts from the medical doctor—at least from the modern doctor's image of himself as a body-mechanic. Freud's physician was to be a student of history, religion, and the arts. Subjects having no connection with medicine, and which never enter the physician's practice, such as "history of civilization, mythology, the psychology of religion, and literature," were to be storehouses from which the psychoanalyst would borrow select pieces of truth in defining symptoms. The first and permanent Freudian task was not empirical research but interpretative rearrangement of the intricate jumble of data accumulated by the cultural sciences.

A good idea of Freud's professional ideal may be gathered from his defense of lay analysis (1926). During the late twenties and early thirties the psychoanalytic movement was split by the question of whether those without scientific ordination—the M.D.—were to be encouraged, or even permitted, to become analysts. In urging that the practice of psychoanalysis should not be limited to physicians, Freud differed with the majority of his followers. At the time of the controversy, four-fifths of the practicing analysts were medical doctors. The psychoanalyst, in Freud's opinion, must not allow himself to become simply another specialist in the medical profession. In his relation to patients, the analyst cannot avoid taking over the charismatic capital of the religious healer; he becomes, if he is a good clinician, "a secular spiritual guide." There are, in Freud's papers, traces of his fantasy life as a messianic figure, momentary visions of an analytic priesthood. This, despite the simoniacal terms of the analytic pedagogy, and its growing respectability—but then Freud was certain that his secular guides would not be hurt by simony. In the world as he understood it, money made men talk seriously and respectfully to those whom they paid to listen.

Freud's struggle against being "swallowed up by medicine" has been— at least in America, the country most receptive to Freudianism—little heeded. Although psychoanalysis has not, as he feared, been shelved in "textbooks on psychiatry in the chapter headed 'Therapy,' next to procedures such as hypnotic suggestion, auto-suggestion, and persuasion," the American psychoanalytic movement has taken the cover granted by the medical profession. Freud had something different in mind—a movement which would obtain the approval of the community and yet remain somehow superior to financial or professional success. The present generation of analysts cannot be blamed for betraying Freud's ideal. They came into a movement that had already become a profession. Their energy and imagination as a group shows up creditably in relation to the larger profession with which they have identified themselves. Surely the analysts cannot be blamed for failing to accomplish what intellectuals in our society find increasingly difficult—to catch the public ear, and still not become hired critics, entertainers in the negative. Liberal culture has shown its power not so much in the marginal freedom it allows dissenters as in its capacity to absorb—without the slightest indigestion—and even canonize its critics. Witness the enduring vogue of that acerb master Freud himself. The currents of American unbelief shift to carry along every critic. The analysts did not make the moral revolution in America; in fact they have been called into being by that very revolution, which, if not world-wide, is at least epidemic in the West. Now the analysts must perform a conservative function: that of getting their patients safely past those crises of identity that follow upon the failure of identification with the old authorities, which have not succeeded in maintaining themselves. When there is only enough fight left in a belief to hurt the believer, analysts have no choice except to help their patients to a truce with their unbelief.

Freud himself foresaw the rapidity with which his doctrine would become acceptable, the cure thereby becoming part of the disease. This insight lies behind his acrimonious deprecations of America and of the potential popularity of psychoanalysis in this culture. His uneasiness was even better expressed by his rather shrill insistence that true adherents to analysis must not merely have given intellectual assent but have come to their therapeutic belief after overcoming strong resistance. Anyone who has been disturbed by the multiplication of therapeutic beliefs current in America will know the uneasiness out of which Freud made his demand for resistance.

The word "therapeutic" needs amplifying. Therapy implies an intention to convert, to criticize one way of life and to work toward another. Of course, patients ought not to learn psychoanalysis but about themselves; nevertheless the patient comes away with an experience of the doctrine that underlies the therapeutic encounter. The profound subjectivity of the doctrinal experience, where successfully absorbed, makes Freudianism immune to the dialectic of its own criticisms. There are loyalty and faith here, as well as a point of view. Psychoanalytic criticism does not set itself up to be criticized, feeding yet another ambiguity into the crisis of identity. So far as it clears away the residual identities that make people ill, Freudianism does not thereby destroy its own capacity to forge a new identity, for it helps bring to life what is essentially a counter-identity. Once the patient is free of the last authority, the therapist, he has achieved the only possible and real freedom; he is himself alone—however diminished that self may be. Thus are disengagements masked as liberations, modest encouragements to life for its own sake proposed as an ideal of freedom.

Freud's recognition of therapy as a moral pedagogy was paralleled by a shift in the type of patient psychoanalysis attracted. In the beginning psychoanalysis was not so exclusively scientific homiletics. Though the patients Freud treated did disclose doubts about what to do with their lives (for instance, "Lucy R."), there were always tangible symptoms—a paralyzed leg, a hand-washing compulsion, impotence—by the resolution of which one could certify the cure. Yet the transition from the uninformed patient, suffering limited and objective symptoms, to the informed patient, perhaps symptomless except for his acute sense of suffering, is forecast in Freud's own writings. To find the humdrum behavior of everyday life psychopathological, as Freud did, is to move nearer that excitement of the wholly interesting life that characterizes the nineteenth-century Romantics' attempt to escape precisely the humdrum in experience. All experience is symptomatic now. People seek treatment because they sleep poorly, or have headaches, or feel apathetic toward loved ones, or because they are dissatisfied with their lives. Patients complain of the boredom and vacuity of their inner freedom, and desire to learn how to fill it by means of strategies that guarantee more direct satisfaction. In response to the increasingly diffused complaints of patients, psychoanalysis has had to grow more openly didactic. Conversely, because of its increasingly ideological bent, psychoanalysis may be said to be partly manufacturing its own clientele. As the aristocratic Roman summoned his philosopher when he was ill, as the Christian went to his pastor, so the dispirited modern visits his analyst. But the psychoanalyst does not compete with older therapists; his is not a therapy of belief but one which instructs how to live without belief.

Freud developed his sense of the times and of the place psychoanalysis had in them from the crude positivist chronology. History had moved to the last of the three stages: from (1) cohesive societies of primitive man, a system of repression implemented by taboos, to (2) religious cohesions, a culture of repression upheld by theologies, to (3) modern culture, an era in which the old repressions are being loosened but not yet superseded. Freud's work would lose in coherence without the positivist estimate of a contemporary crisis of belief. The "extraordinary increase in the neuroses" could only be understood, he thought, as the accompaniment to the failure of normative authority; it was the inevitable price mankind pays during the transition between waning moralities and the healthy indifference of science, as such, to all moralities. A culture extricating itself from religious constraints is bound to carry habits of constraint into the new, wider world. Its condition is still post-religious, its freedom still negative. Religion can no longer save the individual from forming his private neurosis, for he has become his own religion: taking care of himself is his ritual now, and health is the ultimate dogma. With the end of religious community, the sects become countless, each with a membership of one. Freud's conception of nervousness is intimately bound up with his critique of religion in its last phase, long after it has ceased to multiply our diseased individuality into collective health. Marking the "intensity of people's inner lack of resolution and craving for authority," Freud thus interpreted Western religion in its waning phase.

   Though the intent of therapy is ostensibly to show the patient how to live without belief, the ideological effect of psychiatric treatment, and of the wider therapy of Freudian doctrine, is surely to replace the moral irresoluteness fostered by the decline of religion with a new theoretic resolution. Indeed, no scientific theory about religion has ever been disinterested: the substitution of theory for belief is one of the highest achievements of secular scientific culture. It is in this sense that Marxist theory functions as a substitute for religion. While analyzing established modes of belief as ideologies, Marx advanced a counter-belief that is at the same time his critical scientific theory. Counter-beliefs may become the basis of new ideological communions, as, for example, those withdrawn sects which are organized in self-conscious opposition to the remainder of Christendom. The Communist movement shows this exclusivist sectarian character, with capitalism cast in the role once played by Christendom—except that the Communist movement, as the last capitalist sect, has developed the characteristics of a universal church. Psychoanalysis creates little communions of counter-belief; more accurately, Freud mixed belief with theory, to create therapeutic communities of two.

II

We see in his consciousness of the decline of belief how much of a social and historical theorist Freud was. It is important to appreciate his thought historically to this extent: no more detailed attack on the overcivilized has ever been mounted. It is with the peculiar effect of modern "civilized" morality (Freud indicates his irony by putting "civilized" in quotation marks) that psychoanalysis is concerned. The nervousness of modern man, he maintained, was unique among the kinds of nervousness induced by civilization. Though he had not heard of J. Alfred Prufrock and would scarcely have approved the poet's diagnosis, Freud was certainly aware of that patient's disorder. Prufrock was a neurasthenic. Modern "civilized" morality, being itself hollow, had hollowed him out. If, as Eliot depicts him, Prufrock could not react energetically to the great war, nor to the chatter of frigid ladies in the drawing rooms, it was a symptom of his moral uncertainty. The knowledge that all decisions are his to make had left Prufrock tired and cynical. One of Freud's earlier manifestoes on culture, the essay "'Civilized' Sexual Morality and Modern Nervousness" (1908), is in fact an analysis of the whole class of irresolute Prufrocks who seemed to him the characteristic neurotic personality types of our time.

Entertaining, for the sake of argument, the long-familiar idea that neurosis issues from the clamor and competitiveness of "the modern civilized life," Freud even makes the stock point about stolid rural folk declining in the city. "Neurosis attacks precisely those whose forefathers, after living in simple, healthy, country conditions, offshoots of rude but vigorous stocks, came to the great cities" and reached a higher plane of "cultural attainment." He quotes some familiar critiques which link our "exhausted nerves" to the unremitting strain of urban culture. "Our ears are excited and over-stimulated by large doses of insistent and noisy music. The theaters captivate all the senses with their exciting modes of presentation; the creative arts turn also by preference to the repellent, ugly, and suggestive." Echoing the indictment customarily offered by cultured Europeans, Freud asserts that the strident and materialist American civilization breeds an especially high proportion of neurasthenics. But all this, he argues, however true, is "insufficient to explain in detail the manifestations of nervous disturbance." The "increasing nervousness" of the present day is due to more than external causes—the fact that modern life carries "excitement into far wider circles than formerly." It is in this statement that Freud anticipated the more sociological psychoanalysis of the neo-Freudians: neurosis comes from the peculiar strains and complexity of modern civilization. But he had no sooner taken up this explanation than he rejected it. Freud explained neurosis with more direct polemical effect, as the expression of antagonism between individual and culture: not the result of a one-way impress of society upon the individual, but rather of the "opposition" between the individual constitution and "the demands of civilization."

A patient of his once summed up the matter: "We in our family have all become nervous because we wanted to be something better than what with our origin we were capable of being." Neurosis is the penalty for ambition unprepared for sacrifice. It was not at our traditional ethical ideals as such that Freud launched his attack; to these he offered the highest tribute—his personal adherence. The important gap that he wanted closed was the one between declining traditional codes of behavior and rising demands by the individual for a greater share of happiness now, as quickly as he can learn how to get it. Their sensual energies drained off in endless moral rearmaments, modern "civilized" men have made themselves nervous from too many self-demands.

The morality that gave civilized nervousness its particular quality for Freud was what other culture-critics have named "middle-class." Freud aimed his critique not so much at "peoples" as a whole as at certain "classes." The forensic attachment of psychoanalysis to the problems and anxieties of the cultivated middle classes, uneasy in their refinement, has from the beginning lent a certain bias to its insights into the nature of illness.

Their marriages seemed to Freud to expose the misery of the middle classes. Behind its monogamous façade, marriage among them is eroded by status constraints and social ambition, by a characteristic "anxiety for the consequences of sexual intercourse" which "first dissipates the physical tenderness of the married couples for each other," and turns the subsequent "mental affection between them" to bitter hostilities. Freud judged married love among the middle classes impossible. "Under the spiritual disappointment and physical deprivation which thus becomes the fate of most marriages, both partners find themselves reduced again to their pre-conjugal condition"—abstinence—"but poorer by the loss of an illusion." Indeed, the illusions of purity on which middle-class children are nurtured, Freud argues, create that impotence of men and frigidity among women which he considered endemic in the love-life of the civilized. Freud closes his great essay on modern nervousness with an urgent appeal for the reform of the prevailing "civilized" morality.

This appeal for reform is nowhere made specific, being embedded in his analysis of sexual affection as such. By his anatomizing of the erotic process, Freud reinforced on a theoretic level the very process of disenchantment that had made love so quick and disappointing. The erotic life, like the economic, becomes under Freudian guidance an area for methodical self-examination and systematic improvement, until finally love itself is a field for reason to conquer. In this sense, although Freud is critical of middle-class moralism, he himself may be charged with being very middle-class in his moral attitudes. His emphasis is on the economics of emotion; from it proceeds his injunction that some hoarding of affect is necessary to health. The analyst may be seen as an investment broker of the emotions.

Criticisms of the overcivilized classes seem to me debatable so far as they depend on the period envy of lower-class vitality. . . . It is fitting that Freud's earliest recorded musing on the pathos of the refined classes—it dates from 1885, when he was twenty-seven—occurred in Paris, during a performance of *Carmen*. In a letter to his fiancée, from whom he had been separated during a long engagement, Freud reports on how, watching the opera, he was reminded of the disposition of the civilized to deprive themselves. "The mob give vent to their impulses," they love and hate uninhibitedly, while

> we economize with our health, our capacity for enjoyment, our forces: we save up for something, not knowing ourselves for what. And this habit of constant suppression of natural instinct gives us the character of refinement. . . . Why do we not get drunk? Because the discomfort and shame of the hangover gives us more "unpleasure" than the pleasure of getting drunk gives us. Why don't we fall in love over again every month? Because with every parting something of our heart is torn away. . . . Thus our striving is more concerned with avoiding pain than with creating enjoyment.

It is different, Freud assumes, with the "common people." Beset by direct social hardship, they cannot afford the luxury of such complex individual feelings:

> Why should they feel their desires intensely when all the afflictions nature and society have in store is directed against those they love: why should they scorn a momentary pleasure when no other awaits them? The poor are too powerless, too exposed, to do as we do.

Fear of too much sensibility has been a standard anxiety of the educated since Rousseau. Characteristically, it goes along with an ambivalent attitude toward the lower classes—part disdain for their being rude and unrefined, and part envy for their not having to carry the burden of culture.

Personal sympathy for the lower orders was balanced by Freud's professional concern with the higher. Exhausted as they were by "restrictions on sexual activity" together with "an increase of anxiety concerning life and . . . fear of death," the civilized classes, he thought, were gradually excluding themselves "from participation in the future." Although Freud does note among the civilized "a diminished inclination to beget offspring," their fate is sealed for reasons other than Malthusian. They have reduced their "capacity for enjoyment," and correspondingly, have become timid to the point of being unwilling "to incur risk of death in whatever cause." A fear of overcultivation far more desperate than Freud's drove Nietzsche to his deepest nightmare: of the "last man," whose posture is reclining, whose feeling is ennui. Freud's last man would be not so much bored as debilitated, exhausted by the struggle to live beyond his psychological means, suspicious of his own moralism. In a way that Freud has oddly abetted, the civilized have grown keenly aware of their repressions and spend much time coping with them. The sense of political defeat that prevails in the West arises in part from a more general feeling shared by figures as different as Freud and Ernst Troeltsch: that fresh social energies can come only from the bottom of the culture-class hierarchy.

Suppose the civilized were to become trained in the detection of their own repressions? It is, after all, on the ears of the civilized, always alert to the burdens of civilization, that arguments against repressive culture have fallen most persuasively; the masses never need persuading. To make delicacy of feeling, not the lack of it, the problem of our health discloses how near the Freudian psychology drifts to a sophisticated primitivism. The continuing celebration of Freudianism demonstrates how viable a primitivist ethics remains in America. For reasons of libidinal economy, some of the heavier investments in culture will have to be written off. Thus Freud shatters the humanist hope that high culture itself may succeed religion as a source of moral controls.

III

However much, as a man of culture, he personally loathed barbarism, Freud gave it a certan therapeutic sanction. Believing that there are "many more hypocrites than truly civilized persons," he shared an image widespread in the era succeeding the prudish—that phoenix image of a better culture rising out of the ruins left behind by a resurgent barbarism. Violence could be a useful cathartic, medicine to an over-refined society. This is the meaning, as I read it, of Freud's oracular "Thoughts for the Times on War and Death."

The holder of these "Thoughts" was a man of culture who has transcended his own delicacies and inhibitions momentarily, to remark on their naïveté. The tone is Olympian. Yet plainly World War I alerted Freud's imagination. "People really die . . . often tens of thousands in a single day." Freud experienced the war as a painful chastisement of those "citizens of the civilized world" who had been confident that base patriotisms had been replaced by "enjoyment of this common civilization." He tried to explain to the refined what generosity had enlarged their illusions; "In reality our fellow-citizens have not sunk so low as we feared, because they had never risen so high as we believed." Freud accused Europe of developing, in the pre-1914 era, a timid "museum" culture, caring only to preserve its facades intact. European culture, consisting too much of "please do not touch" signs placed discreetly around reality, discouraged passion and excitement. A trained incapacity to accept reality, in particular death, limited the insights and actions of the cultured. Civilized morality had tended to "put death on one side." When the "highest stake in the game of living, life itself, may not be risked," life becomes impoverished, uninteresting. Civilized life be-comes—here Freud used one of his more tendentious metaphors—"as shal-low and empty as . . . an American flirtation, in which it is understood from the first that nothing is to happen, as contrasted with a Continental love-affair in which both partners must constantly bear its serious consequences in mind." A more studied appreciation of death could reinstruct us in the serious consequences of living, Freud believed. As an alternative to the supine figure representing the ennui of the civilized, he envisioned one fixed in a stoic posture, dressed in a German uniform. It is war, he said, which will "sweep away" this enervating "conventional treatment of death." War returns us to our sense of reality. "Death will no longer be denied; we are forced to be-lieve in it."

I do not mean to exaggerate this profound eccentricity among Freud's ideas. The notion of rebarbarization is nowhere near the center of his thought. The therapy of war is admittedly an apocryphal item in the Freudian canon, but the arraignment of culture, which excited such a remedy, is fundamental to his thought. Not only is culture unrealistic, so far as it removes us from death, but it is the cause of emotional fatigue, that charac-teristic form of neurosis among the civilized. Freud charges cultural aspiration and the neglect of instinctual realities with being themselves responsible for cultural regression. Moral inflation ultimately induces moral depression. The "resulting tension" of the "unceasing suppression of instinct . . . betrays itself in the most remarkable phenomena of reaction and compensation." Thus it is civilized morality that breeds war. War became for Freud a massive balancing of the psychic budget, bringing ethically bankrupt humans back to living within their means. Though war may seem to the cultured a "regression," some regressions may be therapeutic. War drew away the superficies of culture; it "has the advantage of taking the truth more into account, and of making life more tolerable for us once again." War and revolution (they amount to the same thing, for Freud, since both have the same regressive character) were natural therapies for the over-civilized, as psychoanalysis was an artificial one.

Respecting as he does the laws of cultural development, Freud does not neglect a more optimistic possibility: that of a drift toward permanent peace. His rhetorical question to Einstein in the famous letter "Why War?" (1932) intimates this other, more hopeful sort of development. "Why do you and I . . . rebel so violently against war?" Freud inquires. "After all, it seems quite a natural thing, no doubt it has a good biological basis and in practice it is scarcely avoidable." In Freud's answer there is promise of a new world led by a third Adam in whom the instincts have been entirely reshaped by rational tutelage. "The main reason why we rebel against war is that we cannot help doing so." The truly civilized, such as Freud and Einstein, develop a "constitutional intolerance of war."

Congenital pacifism, Freud thought, was not a serious possibility for any except a handful like himself. A rational nature was for him at best a "utopian expectation." Some few truly civilized may have no need of therapeutic regressions: most people need the relief supplied by war "from the constant pressure of civilization." Freud put his question squarely to the cultured, imperiled by mass barbarism and yet themselves suffering from the burdens of culture. For our health,

> is it not we who should give in, who should adapt ourselves to war? Should we not confess that in our civilized attitude towards death we are once again living psychologically beyond our means, and should we not rather turn back and recognize the truth? Would it not be better . . . to give a little more prominence to the unconscious attitude towards death which we have hitherto so carefully suppressed?

It was 1915 when Freud acknowledged the collective reassertion of the death-wish. But just because death threatened and the complacencies of peace were blasted, "life has, indeed, become interesting again; it has recovered its full content."

That an intellectual whose maturity fell within the forty years of European peace between 1870 and 1914 should assign a certain positive value to war is not surprising. Even that war was not quite total, and the chief weapons not yet ultimate ones. Still, it is depressing how many intelligent minds have held a hope for culture that involves the notion of sweeping things clean. Such an idea has appealed most obviously to totalitarian intellectuals, but it also has given pleasure to a mind as clear as George Orwell's. After watching British soldiers board troop trains, Orwell hopefully wrote in his diary: "How much rubbish this war will sweep away. . . . War is simply a reversal of civilized life; its motto is 'Evil be thou my good,' and so much of the good of modern life is actually evil that it is questionable whether on balance war does harm."

Freud's sanguine interpretation of a culture dying to liberate individual energy has, I think, repugnant implications. There have been such things as overdeveloped cultures, breeding exquisites among the few while living on the brutalized many. But it is a desperate optimism that believes culture can be improved by diminution. Freud adduces in support the analogy of neurotics freed from the burdens of their accumulated memories. Analogy is never enough. Culture, indeed, needs corrective devices. But destruction is not correction; war creates nothing, releases nothing. The therapy of barbarism is perhaps the most dangerous form of the long-standing resentment of the cultured against themselves.

IV

Despite his criticisms, Freud was not unsympathetic to the old moralities. As a man of culture, he could admire the repressions. But, as a man of science, he had learned from case after case that "what the world calls its code of morals demands more sacrifices than it is worth." Society is not

> sufficiently wealthy [or] well-organized to be able to compensate the individual for his expenditure in instinctual renunciation. It is consequently left to the individual to decide how he can obtain enough compensation for the sacrifice he has made to enable him to retain his mental balance. On the whole, however, he is obliged to live psychologically beyond his income, while the unsatisfied claims of his instincts make him feel the demands of civilization as a constant pressure upon him.

The tension between instinctual candor and cultural hypocrisy, which is the most general cause of the present human illness, must be acknowledged; the act of doing so describes for Freud the beginning of new health. A suspicion of falsehood is, of course, the negative preparation for any conversion. Psychoanalysis, however, demands a special capacity for candor which not only distinguishes it as a healing movement but also connects it with the drive toward disenchantment characteristic of modern literature and of life among the intellectuals.

Freud found the essential lie upon which culture is built in its zealous but faltering repressions. His way of mitigating them was, first, through rational knowledge, and, second, through a prudent compromise with the instinctual depths out of which rational knowledge emerges. He proposes that

> certain instinctual impulses, with whose suppression society has gone too far, should be permitted a certain amount of satisfaction; in the case of certain others *the inefficient method of suppressing them by means of repression should be replaced by a better and securer procedure.*

To replace inefficient moral commitments, Freud offers as a better and securer standard what I call his "ethic of honesty." This honesty Freud would have us achieve by working through the layers of falsehood and fantasy within us to a superior accommodation to reality.

We first meet the ethic of honesty in characteristic Freudian guise—as a merely therapeutic rule. He tells us that, at the very beginning of therapy, the patient must promise "absolute honesty." All facts and feelings are to be laid bare. Not even names can be excepted from communication. Honesty, we learn, is "the fundamental rule of the psychoanalytic technique." But what appears as a rule of therapy is actually a general cultural recommendation.

It is a measure of the negativity of Freud's ethic that he illustrated it by a "just suppose" story, a parody of the reticent manners and morals of the cultivated classes of the nineteenth century. It is a kind of modern pendant to the story of Adam and Eve, pointing to a new garden where honesty has supplanted false innocence. Suppose, Freud writes,

> a number of ladies and gentlemen in good society have planned to have a picnic one day at an inn in the country. The ladies have arranged among themselves that if one of them wants to relieve a natural need she will announce that she is going to pick flowers. Some malicious person, however, has got wind of this secret and has printed on the programme which is sent round to the whole party: "Ladies who wish to retire are requested to announce that they are going to pick flowers."

Freud is that malicious person, with the clear negative spirituality of an unbeliever fascinated by the pathology of belief; the ladies represent culture, made dishonest by the process of repression. Of course (as the story goes), after this disclosure

> no lady will think of availing herself of this flowery pretext, and, in the same way, other similar formulas, which may be freshly agreed upon, will be seriously compromised. What will be the result? The ladies will admit their natural needs without shame and none of the men will object.

Thus in a story Freud published his ethical intention. We must accept our "natural needs," in the face of a culture which has censored open declarations of natural need. In championing a refreshing openness, Freud disclosed the censoring of nature, thus to ease the strain that had told upon our cultural capacities.

What makes neurotics talk is "the pressure of a secret which is burning to be disclosed." Neurotics carry their secret concealed in their talk—"which, despite all temptation, they never reveal." Freud set out to hear this talk, root out the secret from within man, and hold it up before him to inspect and acknowledge. Freudianism was to be indiscreet on principle. "Disclosure of the secret will have attacked, at its most sensitive point, the 'aetiological equation' from which neuroses arise." The new revelation "will have made the gain from the illness illusory; and consequently the final outcome of the changed situation brought about by the physician's indiscretion can only be that the production of the illness will be brought to a stop." Thus Freud reversed, once again, the usual conception: man's chief moral deficiency appears to be not his indiscretions but his reticence.

> The psychoneuroses are substitutive satisfactions of some instinct the presence of which one is obliged to deny to oneself and others. Their capacity to exist depends on this distortion and lack of recognition. When the riddle they present is solved and the solution is accepted by the patients these diseases cease to be able to exist.

Such treatment by mutual self-exposure Freud considered quite extraordinary: "There is hardly anything like this in medicine, though in fairy tales you hear of evil spirits whose power is broken as soon as you can tell them their name—the name which they have kept secret." What is for Freud "repression," psychologically understood, is "secrecy," morally understood. Secrecy is the category of moral illness, for it provides a hiding place for false motives. It is our secrets, hidden from ourselves, that fester and infect action. Thus the entire therapeutic undertaking, based as it is on the promise of "absolute honesty," becomes "a lost labour if a single concession is made to secrecy." For secrecy provides the self with, in Freud's appropriately religious image, a "right of sanctuary" for disreputable citizens of the mental underworld. There are to be no refugees from honesty in Freud's program. He "once treated a high official who was bound by oath not to communicate certain State secrets, and the analysis came to grief as a consequence of this restriction." I have referred [previously] to the tyranny of psychology. In a period of political repression, human concerns often turn inward upon the most private aspects of living. Freud has reinforced this turn toward privacy and the inner life. But he has also helped make inwardness a symptom instead of a salvation. The inquisitiveness of psychology is tyrannical—and shareable.

Freud himself and many others following him, both disciples and detractors, linked psychoanalysis to the religious confessional. Actually, all groups have some mode of confession. But Freud's rule of honesty has a special condition. Psychoanalysis claims not merely to know all, but also—acting on a principle unlike any in the therapeutics of Christian culture—to tell all. It is essential to the Church, as Pius XII has declared, that the secrets of the confessional can on no account be divulged "even to a doctor, even in spite of grave personal inconvenience." For Freud it is therapeutically desirable that the entire society learn the secrets of the analytic couch. The new psychological man would be able quickly to detect dishonesty (or fantasy) in others. This in itself would act premonitorily against withdrawal into illness. It would hasten the "change-over to a more realistic and creditable attitude on the part of society." When relatives, friends, and strangers from whom neurotics

> wish to conceal their mental processes know the general meaning of such symptoms, and if they themselves know that in the manifestations of their illness they are producing nothing that other people cannot instantly interpret,

the disease has lost its essential function as an escape mechanism. Neurotics are too private, too reticent. By proposing to eliminate secrecy, Freud curiously reasserted the hegemony of public morality over private. "Tolerance of society," Freud wrote, "is bound to ensue as a result of psychoanalytic enlightenment." Yet despite the Freudian emphasis on tolerance, this unfolding of the inward life cannot help but mean an increase in the power of the community as well.

What recourse, Freud asks, will people have "if their flight into illness is barred by the indiscreet revelations of psychoanalysis?" His answer hints another kind of civilization, one that is not built on reticence or hypocrisy: they will have to "confess to the instincts that are at work in them, face the conflict, fight for what they want, or go without it." No more forthright assertion of the nature of freedom has ever been made. Freud did not glove the fist that symbolizes freedom, nor mistake it, as liberals often do, for the helping hand.

The ethic of honesty arose early in the middle-class era, and has been characterized by the modesty of its moral demands. "When one wants to eulogize someone," a French preacher of the eighteenth century explained, "one says: he is an honest man. But one never says, one dares not say, he is a true Christian, as if being a Christian were something dishonorable." An *abbé* of the same period describes the ethic of the new class: "You say to us confidently that you are honest men, but that you are not devout. . . . There you have it, my brothers, the eternal refrain, the favorite maxim with which the pretended sages of our century believe they can respond to everything." It is this refrain that Freud perfected. Psychoanalysis has put into fresh expression the hard ethic of honesty, long in process of displacing the religious ethic, which, even as it admitted the universality of sin, proclaimed the inevitability of redemption.

To become candid about his egoism, to defy the admonitions that had made him feel secretive and ashamed of his self-interest, the honest man has needed a science exhibiting the pathology of moral aspiration. This science, however, is based upon a tautological, instinctualist conception of "desiring" or "aiming." Morality derives its energies second-hand, from a process of reaction against desiring. Freud could not speak of the desire to be good in the same sense that he could speak of desiring what we have to renounce for the good. Surely this is one-sided. Aspiration may be as genuine as desire, and as original. Instinctual desire has even been understood as a displacement of frustrated moral aspiration—as it is for some of Dostoevski's demonic characters such as Stavrogin (*The Possessed*) and Velchaninov (*The Eternal Husband*). The English critic V. S. Pritchett has pointed out that George Eliot was perhaps the last great novelist to concentrate on the desire to be good. Since then the passion to be good has become embarrassing, something to which it is better not to admit. To will to be good is anyway a contradiction in terms: the will is never good. Freud can conceive of a person's feeling guilty not because he has been bad but because, as a result of his repressions, he is too moral. This is one source of his influence: his diagnosis that we are sick from our ideals and that the one practicable remedy lies in an infusion from below.

V

The Freudian ethic of honesty is to be preferred to the "sincerity" commended by other nineteenth-century minds perplexed with the problems of waning belief and energy—for instance, by Carlyle in *Heroes and Hero Worship*, Nietzsche in his *Use and Abuse of History*, Sorel in *Reflections on Violence*. Sincerity, in their view, connotes the wholehearted engagement of character. Cherished with equal sincerity, all beliefs become equally meritorious; while "sceptical dilettantism" is held to be the curse of our modern, critical culture. To Carlyle the most repugnant sight is of minds "no longer filled with their Fetish," but given over to mere intellectual conviction. "It is the final scene in all kinds of Worship and Symbolism," Carlyle laments. Jung deplores a similar process in modern culture, in which there is an exhaustion of religious forms and a removal from the emotional depths that energize and justify belief.

For Freud, too, honesty brings one into touch with the emotional depths, where all beliefs are equivalent. But to be in touch with the unconscious is, for him, the supreme mode of heightening self-consciousness, and to accept the equivalence of all beliefs is to dare life without them. Romantic sincerity suspects conscious emotion as shallow, proscribes braggart talk, reverences the rude, inarticulate hero who is in touch with his depths and can draw upon their energies *in action*. And here is where Freud's ethic of honesty differs from Carlyle's or Nietzsche's: in its quasi-cerebral, less activist emphasis on talk, on verbal honesty instead of psychological sincerity. In place of reticence, Freud prescribes talk—thorough, ruthless talk. Honest talk fills the gap in ideals, creates the condition of a new personal integrity. This painful intellectual working-through of illusions contrasts sharply with the romantic conception of honesty as a leap beyond the paralyzing dialectic of illusion and disillusion—into decision.

From this difference between two kinds of honesty we can estimate the gap between the competing psychological ethics of Freud and Jung. Jung is in search of new emotional vitality. His is a situational ethic, based upon increasing the flow of creative energy. Hence he fears too much consciousness as well as too little, and attends particularly to the categories which the unconscious imposes upon conscious expression and which it is the function of the psychologist to discern. Doctrine, myth, works of art all in their plenitude express the vital credulities necessary to the creative life. Hence Jung's interest in the welter of world religions, and his preference for religions that permit welter, as in Asia, to the neater but narrower expressions of Christianity.

Freud, on the other hand, cannot conceive of an excess of consciousness. In this respect, Jung is the more balanced of the two. Energy means to Freud not the capacity for belief but the capacity to reject the swarms of beliefs that return to nag at one—or rather, in the Freudian scheme, to which one returns. Freud's ethic of honesty demands only the negative capacity to achieve and retain unbelief. Of the two ethics, Freud's is the more straitly hostile to religion, although in his too there is a therapeutic simulacrum of faith.

Nevertheless, the Freudian ethic may be liable to an indictment more grave than the verdict of Faith, in the second degree, that has sometimes been read against Jung: the charge of nihilism. As a purely explanatory and scientific ideal, honesty has no content. Though the Freudian training involves intellectual judgment (it is, after all, psycho*analysis*), based on a calm and neutral appraisal of all the demanding elements of a life-situation, still, the freedom to choose must end in choice. Here, at the critical moment, the Freudian ethic of honesty ceases to be helpful.

Being honest, admitting one's nature, does not resolve specific issues of choice. The Freudian ethic emphasizes freedom at the expense of choice. To achieve greater balance within the psyche, to shift the relative weights of instinct and repression, installs no new substantive rules of decision.

In this final suspension, Freud's ethic resembles Sartre's existentialism, which offers a related criterion, authenticity, as a way of judging what is good in human action. André Gide offers lucid disillusionment as the distinguishing mark of humane conduct. But what guarantees that an authentic action, or one conceived in perfect lucidity, will be good or in conformity with human nature? Similarly, after a long process of self-recuperation through lucidity, the Freudian choice may be not more humane but rather more arbitrary. One need not be self-deceived in order to act maliciously. Freud gives no reason why unblinking honesty with oneself should inhibit unblinking evil. Lucidity may render us exquisitely articulate and unapologetic about our aggressions. If, as Freud himself implies, the dangerous energy of the self is guided inward only to prevent a fiercer war without, perhaps the repressed character is still preferable to the honest man. Openness of character may well elicit more, not less, brutality. Unaided by the old transcendental ethics of guilt, or by the rationalist ethics of a future harmony through knowledge, the Freudian lucidity may pierce the deepest shadows of the self without dispelling one degree of gloom.

There is a risk in the ethic of honesty of which Freud is aware. Some lives are so pent-up that a neurosis may be "the least of the evils possible in the circumstances." Some of those "who now take flight into illness" would find the inner conflict exposed by candor insupportable, and "would rapidly succumb or would cause a mischief greater than their own neurotic illness." Honesty is not an ethic for weaklings; it will save no one. Neither will it necessarily render our natures more beneficent. Psychoanalysis prudently refrains from urging men to become what they really are; the new ethic fears the honest criminal lurking behind the pious neurotic. Still, he argued, with all these dangers, his therapy of honesty came modestly priced in a culture where all prices are too high.

Freud's greatness seldom elevates. This was not his purpose. He was a digger, not a builder, an archaeologist of the psyche. Digging at the foundations was the moral mission left to the psychologist after philosophy and religion had raised man too high. According to the Freudian counsel, man must not strain too far the limitations of his instinctual nature. Therefore, knowing, becoming conscious of these limits, is itself a primary ethical act. Consciousness, self-knowledge, interpretative revelation and decision, candor, talking things through—all presume a necessary reduction of ethical aspiration. Without this imperative, Freud's conception of therapy is meaningless. "A little more truthfulness," Freud recommends, instead of the painful old passion for goodness. Psychoanalysis shares the paths of truthfulness common to rationalist doctrines. People ought to be forthright. If they express their true natures, goodness will take care of itself. The ethic of honesty does no more than establish the capacity to break the moral habits into which decisions, once made, tend to form themselves. Freud's is a penultimate ethic tooled to the criticism of ultimates. It regards the disposition of human potentiality as a matter beyond prescription.

As a negative and penultimate ethic, Freud's is dependent on that which it criticizes—ethics that are positive and ultimate. The ethic of honesty presupposes the existence of repressive authority. This psychoanalytic assumption that the traditional moral values of our culture have been inhibitory depends in turn on a more fundamental assumption, now widely accepted in the social sciences: of civilizations as systems of restraint. . . . Freud considered the structure of convictions upon which Western civilization has been operating to be renunciatory in character. Therefore strategies of unbelief, of disclosure, of negation are themselves positive—effecting a studied release of energies heretofore inhibited by the ascetic character of the Western moral system. Honesty is enough only if one assumes, as Freud did, that our real natures have been too much inhibited.

This does not mean that Freud desired an unconditional release of human energies. He is, as I have said, ambivalent toward repressive culture: its major critic and yet defender of its necessity. Given the inability of most minds to be both as critical and as cautious as his own, Freud considered it at least

> a debatable point whether a certain degree of cultural hypocrisy is not indispensable for the maintenance of civilization, because the susceptibility to culture which has hitherto been organized in the minds of present-day men would perhaps not prove sufficient for the task.

Ultimately Freud took the position that the hypocrisies of civilization, being the cause of neurosis, themselves frustrate the purpose of civilization. The neuroses actually represent those socially inimical forces which have been suppressed. Nothing, therefore, is gained by suppression. No advantage is purchased by the sacrifice of mental health. Civilization has a treacherous ally in the neuroses, one that periodically turns against it. Fortunately, from the psychoanalytic point of view, Western culture appears to have lost its capacity to breed charismatic founding fathers, around whose example or teaching new doctrines of compliance may be composed. Of the voices arguing subtly against all possible fathers and the sacrifices they command, Freud's is now the dominant one—antagonist not of this father or that but of the troubling, uniquely human impulse to find a father. His regard for health, at the expense of culture, has been incorporated into the standing American protest against everything past, although he himself protested against the complementary American illusion of a better future. Being a very intelligent protest, Freud's is hidden beneath a science whose very nature as a moral science it denies; for the illness it proposes to treat scientifically is precisely our inherited morality, and therefore it is, in its own terms, both a natural and a moral science.

VI

If Freud takes sides against culture, it is only for therapeutic purposes. He believed no more in instinct than in culture; for his day and age he sought only to correct the imbalance between these two main categories of the moral life. He is the architect of a great revolt against pleasure, not for it. He wrote no briefs for the pleasure principle. Rather he exhibited its futility. It is toward the reality principle that Freud turns us, toward the sober business of living and with no nonsense about its goodness or ease.

Of course the pleasure principle does have an important place in the Freudian scheme, which has led to a false comparison of Freud with the English utilitarians. The resemblance has a certain plausibility. Every action, for Freud as for Bentham, may be tested by the criterion of pleasure, and all actions, being performed, must have been pleasurable enough to be performed. Oral eroticism and mathematics, sodomy and social welfare, low interests and high—all are pleasures. Even suicide pleases the suicide; sadism pleases at least the sadist. Pleasure is, for Freud, identical with motivation in general; there can be no other motive. The "compulsion to repeat," the motive he emphasized after his World War I studies of battle neuroses, appeared to qualify the pleasure principle. Actually, it turned out to be merely another, subtler form of pleasure. The war neurotic repeats his trauma, and if the repetition does not seem to us very pleasurable that is nothing to the neurotic. The pleasure principle is a very subjective one. Further, Freud had a notion of the scarcity of pleasure which seems utilitarian. Each case history detailed the limits of pleasure, its manufacture at home, its expenditure and exchange in the market-place. But emotional rewards are not as scarce in the Freudian economic system as this description would indicate. A fairly unlimited amount of credit exists, in resources untapped by most—in art and learning, in politics and religion—by which pleasure is replenished and new libidinal capital formed outside the home.

Utilitarian psychology led to the respectable ideal anarchism of the nineteenth century—the freedom to pursue one's pleasure so long as that pursuit did not interfere with the pleasure-seeking of others. Freud offered a less optimistic ideal, containing a harder and more internal check. It is the "education to reality," or what amounts to the same thing, the restriction of pleasure, that teaches freedom and at the same time sets the limits of freedom. The reality principle does not completely supplant the pleasure principle, but it tries, through compromise, to exert discipline enough to meet the basic need for efficiency. There is a human reluctance to give up pleasures—especially those of the past—for barely acceptable and certain realities. Psychic illness signifies a clinging to dead pleasures. The neurotic is a coward about life, one who "turns away from reality because he finds it unbearable." Far from advancing the ethical hedonism with which he is mistakenly charged, Freud in his psychology of pleasure indicates the futility of hedonism. Pleasure to him was just the sense of transition from an excess to a deficiency of mental energy. It was a decline in the tension of life, involving a regret as great in its way as the one involved in pain. It followed, then, that death might be the greatest pleasure, and so Freud hypostatized a "death instinct" to complement the erotic instinct. The pleasure principle might more justly be named the principle of pleasure-pain; for, conversely, pain was the transition from a feeling of deficiency to one of excess. Pleasure registers the decrease of pain, a temporary relief from the intensities of living. Freud's description of emotion in economic terms relates less to Bentham's psychology than to the Romantic meta-psychology of Schopenhauer.

Freud's analysis of pleasure must be distinguished not only from utilitarian hedonism but from the prescriptive hedonism of the post-Freudians. Karl Menninger's belief that "psychiatrists should come out squarely and courageously for hedonism as a philosophical position" finds not the faintest echo in Freud. Menninger goes on to quote Rebecca West, with whom he shares the belief that "we need no further argument in favor of taking pleasure as a standard when we consider the only alternative that faces us. If we do not live for pleasure we shall soon find ourselves living for pain. If we do not regard as sacred our own joys and the joys of others, we open the door and let into life the ugliest attribute of the human race, which is cruelty . . . the root of all other vices." If this is indeed the message which "psychoanalysts can and should give to the world," then psychoanalysis has moved a long way from Freud. He understood that cruelty is itself one of the pleasures. No doubt Freud would not have been so confident as some of his followers that the pleasure of being cruel to others—which bestows other, more obvious, pleasures on oneself—would be readily relinquished if pleasure alone were the standard of value. Being an aesthetic result, increasing and decreasing dialectically in terms of the related presence of pain, pleasure is a doubtful value. Thus, contradicting hedonist theory, the Freudian psychology reveals the ephemeral quality of pleasure as an end in itself.

Like his philosophic forerunner Schopenhauer, Freud accepts the essentially contradictory character of reality and preaches a doctrine of resignation to it. Freud's credo is "to endure with resignation"; thus a subtle acceptance of things as they are which changes the very condition to which one is resigned becomes the aim of Freudianism.

In promising patients help and relief through his new therapeutic method, Freud says, he was often faced by this objection: "Why, you tell me yourself that my illness is probably connected with my circumstances and the events of my life. You cannot alter these in any way. How do you propose to help me, then?" And I have been able to make this reply: "No doubt fate would find it easier than I do to relieve you of your illness. But you will be able to convince yourself that much will be gained if we succeed in transforming your hysterical misery into common unhappiness."

It is a curious sort of promise to have attracted so many followers. Common unhappiness is not an ideal toward which one can struggle enthusiastically. But then, the Freudian patient, instructed in the lore of his secret self, is not to become an enthusiast. The therapeutic effort aims at reserving our energies for everyday life instead of having them frittered away in neurosis—or in the analysis itself. Therapy prepares a mixture of detachment and forbearance, a stoic rationality of the kind Epictetus preached. The practiced ease of ex-pected disappointment recommended by Epictetus—beginning with a bro-ken cup, and so on ultimately to one's broken life—is perhaps the best and most classical intimation of Freud's own way of coming to terms with life. To detach the individual from the most powerful lures in life, while teaching him how to pursue others less powerful and less damaging to the pursuer—these aims appear high enough in an age rightly suspicious of salvations. Freud had the tired wisdom of a universal healer for whom no disease can be wholly cured.

Freud never wanders beyond analysis into prophecy. He leaves us with the anxiety of analysis—the anxiety proper to psychological man. Fidelity may frequently be neurotic, but Freud scarcely authorizes adultery. While explaining the incest taboo as a residue of historic repressions, of course he does not sanction the cohabiting of brother and sister, mother and son. Yet if moral rules come only from cultures which legislate deviously for their own advantage, against the freedom of the individual, how can any part of conduct be taken for granted? If every limit can be seen as a limitation of personality, the question with which we may confront every opportunity is: after all, why not? While Freud never committed himself, the antinomian implications are there. And those who have interpreted Freud as advocating, for reasons of health, sexual freedom—promiscuity rather than the strain of fidelity, adultery rather than neuroses—have caught the hint, if not the intent, of his psychoanalysis.

Freud intimates that we are ready for a new beginning; he does not actually suggest one. That there is historical accuracy reflected in this intima-tion we can have no doubt. Better than any other single record, the Freudian text—in its charge of cases, in its incorporation of the pathological ordi-nary—expresses our state of readiness, our sophisticated and much verbalized conviction that the old systems of repressive authority are enfeebled. From this perspective of depth, it is true, Freud undermines the old systems of authority. At the surface, however, this tampering with our repressions may itself foster a new dependence. The new freedom leads to a certain calculated conformity; psychoanalysis finds no more legitimate reasons for being rebellious than for being obedient. It is in this sense that Freudianism carries nihilist implications. A deliberate, detached conformity is more powerful than the old dogmatic varieties, with their exciting illusions of truth beyond matters of motive. Although it claims no validation beyond the pressure of social necessity itself, the present tyranny of psychologizing may well prove more stable than the older enforcements of guilt.

J. H. VAN DEN BERG

Neurosis or Sociosis

THE MEANING OF SYMPTOMS

The year in which the theory of the neuroses and the theory of psychotherapy came into existence out of nowhere can be identified with particular exactness. Both theories appeared in the summer of 1882.

It is a well-known story. In the two years between 1880 and 1882, a Viennese doctor, Josef Breuer, had been trying to gain insight into a disease which had been known since antiquity, but whose symptoms were so capricious and so unstable, and whose physical basis, even after accurate physical examination, appeared so entirely lacking, that nobody knew the outlines of the disease nor the meaning of its symptoms. A young woman—she was twenty-one years old—whom Breuer had been visiting regularly was suffering from this disease. She had a paralysis of the right arm, a disturbance of her eyesight, an annoying cough, and many more symptoms; these symptoms, however, without exception, were characterized by the amazing and in those days entirely unaccountable fact that they were not caused by a defect of a physical nature. Her arm was neurologically sound, even in a state of complete paralysis; the ophthalmologist found no signs of disease in her—nonetheless faulty—eyes; and the throat specialist could not find anything wrong with her throat, in spite of the fact that her cough continued to suggest a physical defect. In addition, she exhibited a remarkable disturbance: she had a tendency to go into a sort of unconsciousness, now and then, for no apparent reason. In such a fit she was not completely unconscious; she answered questions and she was able to take part in conversation. That she had a certain degree of wakefulness was proved by the fact that she made sure

Translated by H.F. Croes. From *The Changing Nature of Man: Introduction to a Historical Psychology*. Copyright © 1961 by W.W. Norton & Co.

that it was Breuer who was with her and nobody else. She felt his hands until she was certain it was he who was by her side. That is to say, all the functions of her waking life had ceased, with this one exception; she could still make contact with her doctor. And as this condition of partial wakefulness was well-known in hypnosis, Breuer named this last symptom "spontaneous hypnosis."

As a result of the talks Breuer had with his patient, he acquired an increasing understanding of the nature of the disturbances, which (and this cannot be emphasized strongly enough) had never before been understood by anyone. His understanding remained fragmentary and vague, however, until, in the summer of 1882, the patient suddenly complained of an entirely new symptom and after a few weeks got rid of it just as suddenly.

This symptom was a sudden inability to drink. Even when eventually she was tortured by a bad thirst, she could not succeed in taking one sip from the glass Breuer offered her. She did bring the glass to her lips; but at the moment they were about to touch the liquid, she fell into a condition very similar to spontaneous hypnosis; and then, apparently horrified, she would put the glass back on the table. Again there were no physical defects.

The explanation of this extraordinary behavior came a few weeks later. Breuer was talking to her while she was in a spontaneous hypnosis; and she suddenly told him, showing evidence of an intense nausea, how she had seen a dog drinking from a glass of a lady, who, ignorant of what had happened, had afterward drunk what was left. She had barely finished her story when she wanted a drink—still in a state of spontaneous hypnosis. Breuer handed her a glass of water; she took it from him, brought it to her lips—and woke up drinking. From that moment the symptom disappeared, and never reoccurred. Breuer's famous note reads, "After she had forcefully expressed her pent-up anger, she wanted to drink and woke up from the hypnosis with the glass at her lips. After this the disturbance disappeared forever."

This sentence indicates the birth of the theories of psychotherapy and of the neuroses, since it embodies the entire explanation of the causes and therapy of neurotic symptoms. And even more: this sentence, which seems so innocent, in any case so very simple, implies a philosophy which is the prevailing philosophy of our society today. Let us see how things developed and what actually happened.

The first publication

In 1893, eleven years after the great discovery, Breuer and his assistant, Sigmund Freud, published a provisional survey of the results of their research. It may be summarized as follows.

1. Every hysteria is the result of an injuring experience—a trauma. An experience like the one Breuer's patient had: seeing a dog drink from a glass of a

lady, who afterward drinks from it herself. An unbearable experience.

2. This experience (of which the hysteria is the result) must be so unbearable that it cannot be included in the totality of life, it cannot be digested. As a result the experience becomes non-participating; it becomes subconscious, or rather, it is pushed into a subconscious state; the experience is pushed out of consciousness.

3. What has been pushed aside, however, does not cease to exist. The experience existed intensely; it was loaded with emotion. And it is just because so much emotion was involved, just because this experience was so intense, it could not be fitted in with the totality and had to be put aside. Can what is repressed protest, but not make itself known? This seems to contain a contradiction. If one harbors a revolting memory, sooner or later he will be reminded of it. But that reminder is exactly what should not happen, since he would get ill from the emotion attached. Consequently the revolting memory makes itself known in another way, so different in appearance that it is not recognized. It appears as a symptom. It is better not to drink than to remember by drinking, and remembering, die emotionally. Rather the symptom than the emotion.

4. The symptom disappears "immediately and definitely" if the emotion can be made to express itself.

Breuer's presence

Breuer and Freud soon had to take back the words "immediately and definitely." Apparently it was not as easy as all that to cure these symptoms. Still, the statement was never taken back completely, simply because there was truth in it. Many symptoms did disappear (in the long run and for a certain length of time), if a patient succeeded in recalling the memory and in making the emotion attached to it express itself.

This brings up one question immediately: if it were only a matter of expressing this emotion, why couldn't the patient do it herself? Why didn't she get a few spells of crying and vomiting? Why did she need another person? And not just anybody, either; she needed Breuer. Why did she need Breuer? For it is quite clear that Breuer's presence was a *conditio sine qua non*; the patient felt his hands until she knew it was he, and only then did she start to talk. "She only started to talk, when she had convinced herself of my identity by feeling my hands," writes Breuer; it is obvious that this fact impressed him. Breuer did not know what to do with this observation, however. Neither did Freud. Especially not Freud; his whole work can be read as one great duel with this observation, which was repeated thousands of times later on—the observation that the patient needs somebody, not just anybody, but one particular person. In this sentence of Breuer's is embodied another theory of the neuroses. But it is better not to digress now; this will be discussed more extensively later on.

The theory and the therapy

Using the above four statements, we can temporarily define the theory of the neuroses and the theory of psychotherapy: every neurosis—for it soon appeared that not only hysteria was involved—every neurosis is a traumatic neurosis; that was Breuer's theory of the neuroses. And the therapy: find the trauma, make the patient remember it, and let the emotion be expressed as forcibly as possible.

Symptoms have a meaning

The fact is, that this simple, undeniably psychiatric, that is, medical, scheme very soon led to a general theory of human existence which appeared to be extremely viable and which was accepted by a great many people. We must examine the first three conclusions and think over what they actually mean.

They look innocent enough, these suppositions of Breuer's: every neurosis is a traumatic neurosis; the trauma is subconscious; the result is a symptom. This last assumption solved the secret which had guarded the symptom for ages. The patient who, with sound legs, cannot walk because his legs are paralyzed, is unable to walk because his legs are filled with an emotion which was not permitted adequate expression. He had, for instance, walked to a fatal spot with these legs, a place where he had to hear some extremely unfortunate information. He let the information submerge into his subconscious, and the walk as well; from then on, for the very reason that he no longer knows about this walk, his legs are "the legs of the walk," they refuse to work; the emotion is in them, and the patient cannot walk on emotion. Besides, the chances that he can still hear are slight; for with his ears he heard the bad tidings, and to hear might make him remember them again; he is trying to prevent that, consequently he is deaf—even if the otologist finds nothing to indicate this deafness. And so on. Every symptom has a meaning. What had been a mystery began to make sense.

Everything has a meaning

The conclusion that symptoms have a meaning leads easily to the thesis that *everything* has a meaning. Of course, it is a leap from the strictly psychiatric to the generally human; but who could object to that, once that it was known that there is hardly a borderline dividing the normal from the neurotic? Besides, there is another reason why this formula that everything has a meaning was accepted so eagerly.

Everything has a meaning. When, before Breuer and Freud, if a man moved his leg up and down while he was talking to his wife, and an onlooker asked what the meaning of this leg movement could be, no one would have taken the question seriously. The movement was something that just happened. We have different ideas now. Not much imagination is needed to suspect that the man with the moving leg has a grudge against his wife; he is kicking her out of the room, even if he reduces his kicks to very modest, and, to the uninitiated (are there any left?), innocent dimensions. If a person today finds delight in sucking his pipe long after the tobacco in it has gone out, it is clear even to a layman that he never really left his mother's breast, he is still sucking the nipple. Or rather, he did not suck it enough then, and it is still bothering him; he made the frustrated desire submerge because it was too disagreeable, and it is coming to the surface when he gnaws his pipe, when he lets saliva run into it and then sucks it back. In the past the question whether this sucking and gnawing might have a meaning was simply never raised. Everyone had his peculiarities, and that was all there was to it. If someone then happened to be visually inclined, no one would have wondered why; now it is quite apparent that he is out to see something else in the things over which his eyes so eagerly rove—his mother, for example, who never, in his youth, appeared naked before him.

I could give scores of examples of trivial, so seemingly unintentional, until recently so apparently innocent inclinations, acts, and habits, which, on closer examination, all appear to have a meaning—which is to say, they are guilty. They can be found in every textbook of psychology. Everything has a meaning: the man who forgets something means something by it; the man who makes a mistake in writing is expressing his most secret thoughts; if he arrives at an appointment too early, there is some reason for it; if he arrives too late, that, too, has its deeper meaning.

The meaning is always located in the past

The fact that in each example the meaning is to be found *in the past*, is of particular significance. The man kicks his wife because of incidents already past, and also because of earlier thoughts about these incidents; the pipe-smoker sucks his pipe because of his skirmish with his mother's breast which turned out so fatally. The visuality of the eidetically-gifted descends from frustrations of an earlier desire to peek.

Threatened innocence

Who can feel at ease with all this? Life is full of trivialities—which appear always to have a meaning. And what a meaning! This meaning always escapes *us*; it almost seems a law that it is always somebody else who discovers the apparent meaning of our actions. What he discovers is honorable only by exception. And he is always right. To deny it does not help, for the meaning

is essentially unknown, it is subconscious. We cannot possibly feel at ease
with it. And yet—I am convinced—we accept the idea that everything has a
meaning so eagerly because more than almost any other formula, it makes us
feel at ease.

Dorian Gray's lilacs

> The spray of lilac fell from his hand upon the gravel. A furry bee came and
> buzzed round it for a moment. Then it began to scramble all over the oval
> stellated globe of the tiny blossoms. He watched it with that strange interest
> in trivial things that we try to develop when things of high import make us
> afraid, or when we are stirred by some new emotion for which we can not
> find expression, or when some thought that terrified us lays sudden siege to
> the brain and calls on us to yield.

The words were written by Oscar Wilde in 1891, two years before the
work of the two Viennese doctors. We may presume that they express the
thoughts of a man who had never heard that the meaning of all things was to
be found in the past. Still, these are the thoughts of a man sensitive enough to
hear and understand the language of trivialities.

I cannot know the meaning behind Dorian Gray's interest in lilacs
and in the scrambling bee if I remain true to the idea that everything has a
meaning, true to the opinion that only incidents in the past, and especially
incidents that were broken off in the past, are the bearers of occurrences.
Shall I take it that Dorian's interest has the same meaning as Jonathan Swift's
delight in Lilliput's small creatures and in their crawling movements? that in
this way, he is expressing his own, once frustrated, exhibitionism, and is also
softening a too painful memory of his own birth? (The reader who wishes
more information on this subject is referred to Ferenczi's article on Gulliver
fantasies.)

Trivialities

Lest the reader feel I am leading him on a false track, it may be necessary to
point out that this quotation from Dorian Gray is of exactly the same caliber as
the examples I mentioned before. Dorian Gray is looking at the lilacs the
same way that the man who is having a discussion with his wife moves his leg
up and down. If we imagine ourselves present at their discussion, we might
hear her make a few less than agreeable remarks; the man, who might very
well have incited these remarks, is thinking; he is moving his leg up and
down, and in this movement he locates his thinking. In the same way, Dorian
is looking at the bee in this important moment; he locates himself in the bee,
and in the bee the significance of the moment becomes concrete. Later on,

when he thinks back to this moment, he will say, "I can still see the lilacs and the bee scrambling over them; it was that moment." Just so will the man say, a long time afterward, "I can still see my leg go up and down; I was trying to touch the tablecloth with the tip of my shoe." And if he won't say it, his wife will: ". . . and just as I had said that, you started moving your leg up and down. I had to keep looking at it. I can still see you do it, when I think of that awful moment."

Is it not this trivial moment itself that is significant? The moving leg does contain a meaning, but it does not seem probable that the leg is moved because of what had been in the past. If its meaning must be located some time ago, in the past, the moving leg might embody the sad story of a marriage resulting in mitigated kicks; a more recent meaning behind the moving leg, though still in the past, could be located in the unfriendly remarks the wife might just have been making. It is so easy to assume; the past contains hundreds of incidents, and there are always a few that can carry the task of being the cause. The past so eagerly sucks us away from the present; yet it is the present in our examples that is significant. If it were not the present, then why would the man be observing his foot with so much interest? Why would he be measuring the distance to the tablecloth as if the future of his marriage depended on it? And why would she be inclined to think, "If he touches the tablecloth, it will be all over between us. He did not touch it. Not now either. He did not touch the tablecloth, thank God." The moving leg contains something by itself, a present actuality, now—however much the activity may be connected with the past at the same time, however much it may recall the past.

And the same is true for the pipe. I am reading and I am smoking my pipe. It goes out; I go on reading. Suddenly my attention is caught by a sentence in the book. I look up and gaze at nothing. I am repeating the sentence to myself, I am tasting the meaning of the words, and at the same time I am sucking my pipe; I let saliva get into it and I suck it back, little by little, just as if I were pouring a little meaning into the words, and then sucking it back again, sharper, more biting, closer to the author's intention.

It seems as if I have extracted the meaning of the words out of my pipe. And exactly in the same way did Dorian Gray look at the bee—fascinated, curious, frightened. And yet every movement of the bee in itself can only be good; the bee has no knowledge of Dorian Gray. The bee is grappling with its own idiosyncrasies.

Bee and lilacs: a closed unity

The bee is grappling with its own idiosyncrasies. There is no doubt about that. The bee and the lilacs, and the sun, and Dorian Gray's shadow constitute a closed unity, ruled by laws of its own. An ethologist could tell us all about it; no doubt he could make it clear that the bee acts the way it does because of a number of causes, all originating from the closed unity, bee-and-lilacs. And since this unity is closed, the observer, as observer, is entirely out of it.

Is not the last statement a tautology, though? When I say that the scheme bee-and-lilacs is a closed unity, and then I say that the observer—in this case, Dorian Gray—is not in it, am I not using a condition to the former statement as a conclusion in the latter? Worded like this, it is hardly noticeable. But if I were to say, the incidents of the bee and the lilacs can be explained with the laws contained in the unity bee-and-lilacs; and consequently the observer, as observer (not as shadow) is out of it—then the tautology becomes obvious. It is possible to prove a lot of things in this way. For instance, that Achilles never passes the turtle. First, the time is circumscribed in such a way that for Achilles to pass the turtle is impossible; and from this it is inferred that it is impossible. The conclusion is flawless—yet Achilles still passes the turtle. The demonstration is based on a tautology. And we are not proving anything when we say that bee-and-lilacs are a closed unity, and therefore Dorian Gray is not in it. The latter is a condition, not a conclusion of the observation that bee-and-lilacs are a closed unity.

What are we doing, actually, when we say that bee-and-lilacs are a closed unity? Are we constructing a trap, like the case of Achilles and the turtle? But of course we are setting a trap. It is just as ridiculous to say that Achilles cannot pass the turtle as to say that Dorian Gray is not in it. And just as no one doubts that Achilles does pass the turtle, within a few strides and without the exertion suggested by the infinitesimal calculus, one should not doubt that Dorian Gray is included in the totality by which he was fascinated. In the case of Achilles we say, "We can see with our own eyes that Achilles passes the turtle." In Dorian Gray's case we should say, "Let us use our eyes and see."

Bee and lilacs: an open unity

What we will then see is this: Dorian Gray has just heard a torrent of eloquent, passionate words. Bewildered, he drops the twig. He sees a bee flying over the flowers; it alights and nervously finds its way over the violet blossoms. He watches it spellbound. The route the bee seeks materializes his own search; every movement of the bee is his movement, every stumbling his stumbling. Soon it will fly away; and its flight may be a visible sign of his own failure. Is it not obvious that Dorian Gray is implicated in what he is seeing? Is not his fascination evidence enough for it? The bee, the lilacs, and Dorian Gray are a totality (we only need to look at it)—a totality, however, in which the laws of ethology are not valid. For if they were valid, it would not be necessary for Dorian to look at the bee so expectantly, with such a compelling, wheedling, demanding, imploring expectancy; all this would have been unnecessary. But this is the way he does look at it, and this would be the way we also would look at it in the same circumstances. When we see things this way, we are demonstrating another unity, one of which we are a part. If we should withdraw from it, then the laws of ethology (of biology, of geology, of astronomy, of physics, of chemistry) would certainly again be valid. But our withdrawal is the very condition of these laws.

The laws of nature

Withdrawing from the things means dehumanizing them. Only if we withdraw, can we find the "laws of nature." These exist, however, only in a closed unity, one which does not include us. As a rule, this condition of withdrawal is not mentioned, and therefore it seems that the laws of nature are always valid. But they are only valid in an artificial reality, a reality from which we are excluded. Only tautologies can make them seem valid in our world.

Angels, good and evil

As Dorian watches the bee, strangely fascinated, these laws are absent. At this moment, there are no laws at all. And it is precisely the absence of any laws that is so peculiar to this moment. Nothing is fixed, everything is in suspension, the moment is undecided. (Isn't he holding his breath? Even physiology is suspended; he doesn't even get out of breath.) The bee, however, muddles through this uncertainty and fills the moment—while Dorian Gray holds his breath; in vain, for the bee scrambles on. The eloquent and passionate words have been launched during a gap in time. The bee fills this gap; its industrious search shows Dorian a structure to cover this gap; in the bee he finds his own structure. That is the meaning of this futile occurrence: something guards the secret of the moment, not just a past frustration. A gap appears in reality, and instantly an insignificant incident fills this gap. What does it mean? Nobody knows. This knowledge does not rest with us; isn't that why we expectantly observe this trivial incident? The knowledge lies within the incident. These trivial occurrences decide for us; they contain a secret, if we only wish to see it. They are our angels, our good angels, and our evil angels. *"Dans chaque petite chose il y a un ange."*

Expelled angels

Now it is easy to see what happens to trivial incidents when they are provided with a meaning—*with a past*: the angels have to leave. And they went. Since I know that my pipesucking habit is the result of my frustration over a nipple, I do not feel any need to explore the bitter liquid for understanding; instead of extracting understanding, I would discover a nipple-complex. Do not think that this discovery would cause me anxiety. That only happened in the beginning, about 1900. Since then we have come to know that we all suffer from this complex, more or less, and any shame has been removed. If Dorian Gray had known that his interest in the bee on the lilac blossoms could be reduced to a frustrated craving for a crawling exhibitionism, his interest too would have died. The gap struck in reality by those passionate words would have closed itself. He could have felt at ease, the way we all feel at ease, nowadays, in this gapless, angel-stripped world; there is no place where the secret can possibly show itself. Everything has a meaning, an additional special meaning, a meaning in the past.

The discovery that the symptoms of a neurotic have a past could be so readily converted into a foundation for a general, eagerly accepted, philosophy because it brought us peace of mind. The idea that every human act has a past did, for humanity in general, what the statement that symptoms have a past did for psychiatry. Any symptoms which can be explained are not disturbing. The neurotic who proves, with his paralyzed legs, that he is clinging to a past incident is not disturbing to us; his legs have no story to tell; they function exclusively in the closed unity of the neurotic and his past.

A subconscious meaning

In psychiatry, and afterward in everyday philosophy, the conclusion that human phenomena have a meaning which is located in the past came to have another, an exceptional and far-reaching significance. The past soon was regarded as a past of long ago, and then a past of very long ago; this past originated so long ago, that its owner could not be expected to know it. As far as the owner was concerned, the meaning of the phenomena was unknown or subconscious.

The word *or* here is misleading; it suggests a natural identity, which is lacking. If we conclude first of all—and rightly—that another person (the observer—the psychotherapist, for instance) knows the meaning, and the patient does not, the only possible inference is that the meaning lies within the other person and not within the patient. The subconscious of the neurotic is to be found within the other person. It would be a perfectly justified conclusion: the subconscious is a faculty of the other person. The name "subconscious" would have to be changed, though. But precisely this conclusion had to be avoided. The meaning had to lie within the patient; only then would the symptoms stop being disturbing to us. But how could this be explained? The meaning is within the patient, and yet it cannot be found within the patient. This contradiction has never ceased to defy us. The neurotic is not able to find the meaning of his symptoms, a meaning which to us is so obvious, not even when it is reasonably pointed out to him what the meaning is and where in the past he can find it. He does not know. And yet he must have this knowledge; if not in the customary way, then in a shape of "not-having" it; that is, subconsciously. The discovery that every symptom has a meaning appears to lead irresistibly to a second discovery, certainly not less significant: the discovery that the patient, apart from having a conscious reason, also and especially has a subconscious reason for his illness. The discovery that every symptom has a meaning leads to the separation of conscious and subconscious.

No sexuality

In their "Provisional Survey" of 1893, Breuer and Freud do not discuss the patient's sexuality. This fact is the more remarkable because it is well-known how just this sexuality was accentuated later on. In 1896, three years after the initial publication, Freud writes that with *every* patient, or even with *every* symptom of *every* patient, one inevitably arrives in the sphere of sexual experiences. Experiences of no pleasant nature, for that matter; the patients told how they were sexually approached by adults when they were children. Without exception they remembered scenes of being seduced by an adult.

The sexual trauma

The theory of neurotic disturbances was rounded off by this discovery. In childhood—not infrequently in even very early childhood—the neurotic experienced a sexual contact. For obvious reasons this contact could not be digested. Consequently it became submerged in the subconscious and remained there, because it had not been digested. But it did not remain quiet. The sexual contact haunted the patient's subconscious until at last it found a disguise: it appeared as a symptom. In accordance with this theory, the therapeutic advice was: unmask the symptom, make the unmasked memory, with the emotion attached to it, beat a retreat, and—the patient will be cured.

Four questions

Presently we shall see that this logical theory was soon hit by a catastrophe from which it never recovered. In the meanwhile, so many peculiarities have accumulated, that it seems sensible to disentangle them and examine them more closely. The following questions will have to be answered:

1. Why is it that the theory of the neuroses was discovered in 1882 and not earlier? According to Ferenczi, the theory of psychoanalysis was "the

shared discovery of an ingenious neurotic and a clever doctor." But that it should be solely the result of a coincidence, in which an exceptionally ingenious neurotic was treated by an exceptionally clever doctor, can hardly be accepted. Especially considering that the discovery was then assimilated not only by experts but by almost every educated layman within a space of twenty or thirty years, which is very quickly indeed. The wisdom of ages would scarcely have failed to notice something which very soon became a matter of course for a great many people, since a rapid assimilation implies knowledge which must be rather simple and obvious. The question of why this knowledge appeared at the end of the nineteenth century and not earlier is an essential one. Discussing it will make it clear at the same time why this discovery did not come later, either; why not in 1925, for instance.

2. Why is it that the discovery of 1882 immediately resulted in the discovery of the two levels on which an incident can affect a person: the conscious and the subconscious? In other words, why was the discovery of 1882 also the discovery of the subconscious—at first only the patient's subconscious (Breuer's hypnoid theory); then, very soon, everybody's (Freud's theories).

The answer to this question has already been prepared: this discovery gives us peace of mind. If everything that concerns us is placed in a certain order, which is forever directed back into the past, the present ceases to be frightening. There had been danger in the present; but since the present has been given a meaning in the past, it has been allocated to a definite place and is no longer floating around us. Demons and friendly spirits become monuments of the past; they freeze and become milestones.

But this is not the whole story. The duality of conscious and subconscious was not forced on the patient; she came to meet it halfway. The first patient brought it into Breuer's office with her. She passed from her usual state into another existence, which quite rightly could be called subconscious, and which, on first sight, was certainly not more reassuring. It was the patients who demonstrated the subconscious; they started to remember things out of this subconscious; they managed to remember amazing events which were inaccessible until the moment they were treated. And then sane, perfectly normal people showed, with similar abandonment, that they were split in the same way. They acted and dreamt in the scheme of consciousness and subconsciousness. They made mistakes and slips of the tongue, they forgot appointments, and they remembered concealed symbols the next morning. Their existence was like walking and sleepwalking at the same time. It had never been like this before—at least, history does not mention it. But no one accepts this as evidence that the subconscious had not existed before. The usual argument is that it had been there all the time, this subconscious, but nobody noticed. Which elicits the questions: Why did nobody see it? Why, as soon as the first person saw it, did everybody see it? Everybody saw it so clearly that the conscious seemed rather insignificant by comparison.

3. Why was sexuality not mentioned in the first publication, which was, after all, the result of many years of research and of many more years of deliberation? This question is closely related to the next:

4. Why was everything related to sexuality soon afterward? Neuroses, said Freud, are derangements caused exclusively by sexual difficulties. "With a normal sex life, neuroses are impossible," is the thesis in its reverse, just as absolute, form. When, during the last years of his life, Freud pessimistically considered the possibilities of psychoanalysis, he repeated this opinion. The motive which makes a neurotic woman seek medical treatment, he wrote, is ultimately that she has no penis and that she wants to have one. But then, how can she get well? How can a man get well, for that matter; for although he has a penis, he must lose it in order to get well. For is he not obliged to accept his cure from a man (the therapist), and is not this prostration actually a sort of castration?

The question of why everything became related to sexuality concerns us all. For it became apparent, that not only the neurotics, but also the non-neurotics, were determined to a great extent by sexuality. So much so that the new theory was called "pansexualism," an epithet which was repudiated so passionately, that perhaps it might have been well to give a thought to the cause of this passion. What hid behind it, in any case, was a sardonic grin, a grin which meant: Yes, you normal people, you too. It is no good giving yourself airs; even your elevated, spiritual existence is based on whether you have, or do not have, an unimpaired penis.

A fifth question

Before trying to answer these four questions, I must draw the reader's attention to a fifth question, a very simple one. The answer to this will lead us straight to the other four answers. The question is: The discovery occurred in 1882, but the first publication was made only in 1893, eleven years later. Why this long interval? Does the fact that the first publication was called "provisional" perhaps imply there were fundamental motives for this waiting?

Freud answered this last question himself. He waited till 1925 to do so, though, the year that Breuer died. The reason for the delay had been Breuer; he was opposed to publication. His reasons seem naive to us now: the patient fell in love with him and told people in Vienna that she was pregnant by him. No modern psychotherapist would be worried by such a story, but in those days, psychotherapists were much more sensitive. We are thus brought back to the question, what was wrong with sexuality in those days? Why was Breuer so upset when this subject was broached? Why was everybody so horrified, so indignant, so angry, when Freud confronted people with it? The whole civilized world pounced upon him, tried to annihilate him, to shut his mouth, to prevent him crying out so loudly what had to be kept silent at all cost.

Breuer knew that their publication of 1893 had been misleading. The patient was in love with him; he must have noticed. She told him that she was pregnant; he should have mentioned it in an objective scientific report. He even knew that every neurosis was a struggle with sex. "It is always bedroom secrets," he had whispered to Freud, when the latter once asked him what he thought was the cause of a neurosis. Later on he could not remember that he had said it; making use of his own invention, he submerged the experience and the statement in his subconscious. But Freud did not forget. He even added another expert's opinion, Charcot's: "*C'est toujours la chose génitale, toujours, toujours,*" noting, at the same time, that Charcot had very little interest in these genital matters.

Something was wrong with sexuality in those days. Things that had to do with sex were not supposed to show themselves, they had to be kept a secret, they had to be kept in the dark; sexuality had come to a dead end. This is apparent in the lapsed eleven years between 1882 and 1893; it is apparent from Breuer's fright and reluctance, which soon turned into his not being interested; it is apparent from the absence of every trace of sexuality in the first publication; and finally it is apparent from the general passionate indignation when Freud brought it into the limelight. Evidently this was not supposed to happen. Sexuality was a masked, enveloped sexuality; one could not permit it to be uncovered. Everyone feared that irrevocable evil would come of it, and each man tried to protect the child, the woman, and finally himself against this evil.

The other questions

The conclusion that sexuality had come to a dead end implies the answers to nearly all our other questions. It explains why nothing of an erotic or sexual nature was allowed to appear. But is also makes plain what happened soon afterward: the discovery that every patient was struggling with sexual difficulties, so that sexuality was mentioned in every publication, and not just mentioned but even discussed at some length is explained—temporarily—by the nineteenth century's derangement of sexuality.

This is no small matter. Sexuality is an essential quality of our human existence, as has been proved beyond doubt by analytical psychology. Moreover, sex is concerned with a contact which, more than any other contact, requires an involvement of the whole personality. Isn't this true? In friendship, for instance, not all our faculties are involved; physical and sexual faculties do not play a prominent part. But in the sexual relationship, all our faculties are involved—at least as long as the sexual relationship fulfills the commonly accepted desiderata. The sexual contact is a complete contact; it fills the days and the years, and it makes the highest demands. Is it not logical that the neurotic—he or she who does not know what to do with life, who makes a Gordian knot of his or her relationships—that such a person runs aground on sexuality? It is almost unavoidable that he will get into difficulties in this area.

But it is still doubtful whether the neurotics of those days would all have landed in sexual difficulties, so completely without exception, and with such general abandonment, if sexuality itself had not been deranged. For everybody: for the entire western civilization. I shall provide evidence for this statement later; now it is more important to point out that a society which permits a derangement of sexuality is in danger.

How can a child grow up sexually if sexuality is kept a complete secret, if it is not allowed to show itself, if it is vehemently forbidden? How can a young adult reach an understanding with the other sex, if its sexuality is absent, and if he, himself, is sexless by social definition? Moreover, how can he be married and beget children, if, at the same time, he has to maintain stubbornly—not only toward society but also toward his partner—that, in a way, there is no such thing as sex? If on anything, the neurotic had to run aground on sexuality. Everyone had more or less run aground on it.

The question why the birthdate of the theory of the neuroses coincided with the discovery of the subconscious can now be answered. The subconscious, in those days, meant sexuality. Sexuality had arrived at a dead end, it was out of the picture, it was not participating, it was—or rather, it had become—subconscious. The neurotic who became entangled with life became entangled, above all, with sexuality. Every observation of the neurotic had to result in a confrontation with sexuality; and as this was exactly what had been put aside, what had been removed from (conscious) life, the discovery of neurosis meant the discovery of the subconscious.

Only one question remains: Why was this discovery made in 1882, that is, at the end of the nineteenth century? Or, in other words, what had happened to sexuality in the nineteenth century? In my opinion this is the most essential question on the theory of the neuroses. Before discussing it, though, it might clarify matters first to proceed with the historical review we left a moment ago.

A disconcerting discovery

By about 1900, the theory of the neuroses was well defined. In short, it was this: The neurotic had been subjected to a sexual approach by an adult when he was a child. The psychical injury sustained by this experience was made subconscious, for safety's sake. After a while, this produced a tension. The injury remained; when the child grew up, it started to hurt. The result was a symptom.

It is obvious: everything depends on the sexual trauma. It is therefore easy to understand why Freud became confused when it appeared that these sexual traumata, described so emotionally by his patients, had also occurred to every non-neurotic known to him with same frequency and gravity. At about the same time, he made another discovery which made him doubt the validity of his theory even more. His words at that moment are mentioned so rarely—and they have such significance—that I will quote them here.

In 1925, when Freud looked back at the many events in his life, he lingered over the year 1900. Commenting upon it, he writes, "When I realized that these sexual approaches had never actually occurred, that they were just fantasies made up by my patients, or perhaps even suggested by myself, I was at my wit's end for some time."

The psychic traumata, which the patient, with the assiduous help of the psychotherapist, managed to remember, and whose remembering effected a vanishing of the symptoms, *had actually never happened.* One really cannot be surprised enough at it. And when normal people started to confess the same sexual traumata, and these stories, too, appeared invariably and with undoubtable clarity never to have been true—then something very extraordinary must have been going on. The sane and the neurotic both complained about nonexistent matters; the neurotic was even ill because of them, suffering from what never happened. What did this mean?

What was happening becomes clear if we take the last remark literally. The neurotic was suffering from what never happened—was he not suffering from a sexuality which had been made absent? To indicate this absence he had to resort to fantasy. "My father touched my genitals"; that was the only way in which the grown girl could say that her father had been an entirely sexless person. She could not say this with these words. What does not exist in any way cannot be expressed. She had to show its absence by a made-up—an absent—presence. But this was not the answer Freud formulated.

The forbidden solution

His correct considerations at this moment should have been these: If every patient and every normal person relates events, and even serious, very serious, events from his past which actually never happened, then something is wrong with that past. The past has become talkative, but it is talking nonsense, it is just playing the fool. For each fact in the present, the past is giving history, but a history which never was, which evidently was made up quickly; the past is fabricating history, it is making up astounding events and indelible experiences. The past would not do this if it had not been forced to do it. Yet, is that not the case, exactly? Is the past not obliged to talk and talk and talk, if the idea that everything has a past is allowed no exception? Apparently there was every reason to make this rule absolute; nineteenth-century man was afraid, he found safety if the "meaning" of things was located in the past. But the past was not yet ready for this task, it was just being built; nonetheless it had to produce a "meaning" for everything. Is it surprising that at the end of the nineteenth century the past started to make up stories?

Eventually the past learned its task. In our day it no longer produces hastily fabricated fantasies. The modern fantasies are much better constructed; so well constructed, in fact, that it is hardly possible to unmask them, if at all. The modern fantasies like "lack of maternal care," "affective disintegration of the family," and so on, have become "true." For the past which learned its task did not learn it just for the fun of it, but out of necessity, the necessity embodied in the irresistible idea that everything has a meaning. Everything is "past"; nothing is "present." Since the present was made uninhabitable by the signs pointing to the past, the past had to take over the task which had been entrusted to the present for as long as man could remember. The past did take over the task; and now we are all living in the past.

Perhaps it would not have been too late to stop this development, at the last moment, about 1900. Freud could have said: "My patients are apparently not ill in the past, they are ill in the present, for it is the present that induces the past to tell lies. Perhaps their stories are meant to take us away from the present, away from where it hurts most." But it was Adler who was the first to express this idea. The neurotic, he wrote in 1912, is not suffering from his past; he is creating it. Jung was the second to say this. In 1913 he wrote, "If we are searching in the past, we are walking into the trap, set for us by the patient. The patient wants to take us away as far as possible from the painful present." It was this statement, among others, which made Jung disappear from the analytical firmament.

Thus, the present was not allowed to remain significant. For the significance of the present—the conflicts, tensions, and fears of life in around 1900—was what made patients ill and normal people not quite normal. The past—after some delay—offered them shelter.

The solution

And so Freud's solution to the impasse of 1900 becomes easier to understand.

Not in the present did he locate the causes of the symptoms, but always further in the past. He who, on principle, resorts to the past is obliged to retreat ever deeper there. For the past has once been present, and for that reason was part of the dangers which exist in the present. Only when the past loses itself in primeval ages, in other words, only when the character of the present has been substantially erased from the past—only when the past has been made entirely imaginary and so unreal—only then is the regression halted.

That is the reason why Freud, when he removed the pathogenic conflict from the childhood years and looked for another time when it could be accommodated more satisfactorily, did not consider the time between ovulation and delivery.

There *are* psychotherapists who think that this time period is important. One needs only to realize what happens during this period to see how easily things can go wrong, especially during these months. First, the future subject as ovum—as half a subject, actually—is thrown out of the secure and cosy ovary. He enters the free abdominal cavity, dangerous because of extrauterine pregnancies. Then an octopus-like tentacle catches the poor wanderer and carries him to an extremely small opening, through which he has to pass. After that comes the journey through the uterine tube, a tight passage, the more anxious because the half-pilgrim never knows whether the army of spermatozoa is approaching or not. If it is not, a scornful death awaits him. But if it is approaching, alarming things will happen. For one of the army is admitted, even though it costs him his tail—castration number one— while the others remain waiting outside, swearing, and the two half-subjects, filled with love, become one.

The primeval scene

This postovular and prenatal theory is not Freud's; some of his followers created it. Although his bound-to-the-past doctrine made this theory, and others like it, possible, he would not have accepted it. Not because it is not true; for what is "true" in these matters? The patients of the psychotherapists who believe in this theory certainly provide enough evidence to support it. They dream of volcanic eruptions, octopi, exhausting journeys over lakes and through narrow passages; they dream about a clash, with themselves, in a guilt-laden atmosphere. No; as far as the *truth* of this theory is concerned, Freud could easily have placed the pathogenic moment in this period. However, this theory would have been too near the present for him. His regression went back much further. This was also the reason why he could not accept Rank's idea that neurotic troubles reverted to the trauma of birth.

Freud put the psychotraumatic moment long before the moment of conception, even before the generation which preceded the conception, so that the connection with the present was entirely lost. He went back to primeval times, when, according to his view, mature sons turned against their fathers, who possessed the women too exclusively. Horrible things happened. Some fathers were killed and eaten; but other fathers managed to avoid this fate, and instead robbed their sons of their genitals. The girls who witnessed these scenes thought, in the confusion of the moment, that they had been castrated at an earlier occasion, which they did not remember. And since those days fathers have been full of suspicion, sons full of fear, and daughters full of shame and envy. And thus children arrive in this world entangled in a heritage of love and hate for their parents. Is it not amazing that not everybody is a neurotic?

By 1912 the principle of this theory of the *Totemmahlzeit* was already present. Freud never abandoned it, not even when ethnological research made it clear that these were untenable fantasies. "The relevant publications are well known to me," he wrote in 1937, "but they have not convinced me. The totem-meal has served me well, and I have never met those who reject it." A haughty answer, but easy to understand if one realizes what it was that led Freud to this theory, which he borrowed from Robertson Smith. This theory, so wrongly called the theory of transference, and the rupture between him and Ferenczi, who had been more faithful than most others, show that above all Freud avoided the present. He did not desire to ascribe any meaning to it.

The consequences of the primeval scene

Patients thus are ill because of the totem-meal; the normal barely escape being ill. The childhood of every child is the evidence. Hardly does the baby have his first tooth than he bites his mother's breast with it; the adults are his enemies from the start. Soon afterward he messes with his feces, teasing his parents and warning his father; for aren't feces a pseudo penis? The father's subconscious does not miss the child's gesture. If the child is a boy, he is sure to touch his genitals sooner or later. Then the father hurls his taboo; the knife is on the way, so to speak. The father need not say a word, his presence is enough; for doesn't the child have a lively memory—even if it is subconscious—of the days when fathers had been less inhibited in their aggression? The girl has nothing to play with; she would like to have it, but all she finds is an absence. And exactly because she discovers that she does lack something, the memory of the primeval scene, of which she had been a witness, awakens in her—subconsciously. She made one mistake then, and she makes another now; she thinks that she has had a penis, but that her father took it from her. From that moment on her whole life is one hopeless struggle to recapture it. At first she finds it again in her feces; knowing her duty she hands it over to her father. Later on she will have a child; but this penis, too, she will give to the man. The poor girl; she struggles with her anatomy in vain.

How easily does the child slip. The first years of life are full of traps; many a child gets caught in them. The girls, especially, have a hard time. More women are neurotics than men—at least this was true in Freud's day.

The second theory of the neuroses

The theory of the neuroses was changed considerably by these ideas. Previously a neurosis was ascribed to a psychotrauma, an injury sustained in childhood. In the new theory, the child is born with an almost hopeless prognosis. It possesses a sexuality which is constitutionally defective; its relationships are corrupted by the totem-meal. Even if there is no trace of a psychotrauma, the child will inevitably get into difficulties. There are many barriers over which it must pass, the most important of which are the "oral phase," the "anal phase," the "phallic phase," the "oedipus complex," and the "castration complex" (the last two in reversed order for the girl); the neurotic is the adult who did not manage to pass all these barriers as a child. If he got stuck in the oral phase, he is "orally aggressive": he has a big mouth, he eats a lot with gusto, and he loves to smoke. Did he get stuck in the anal phase? then he is stingy and conservative, and he is often to be found in the toilet. Some fail to get beyond the oedipus complex; they cannot get away from their parents, they do not marry, or if they do, they find themselves constantly in situations which oddly resemble their childhood. Then there is the neurosis from which every woman suffers (occasionally, men suffer from it too): the castration complex, which expresses itself in a persistent grudge against the male, and in a paralyzing self-disgust. If the neurotic happens not to recognize himself in one of these types, he will benefit from the knowledge that the qualities are often expressed by their opposites; and also, the subconscious commonly shifts a quality from one group to another as a method of camouflage.

It is clear that in this theory the psychotrauma has disappeared; it was too near the present. Now—we should say that this "now," the "now" of the second theory of the neuroses, lies between 1905 and 1920; for a small group of psychotherapists it lasted until 1945; for an extremely small group it is still valid today—now the neurosis originates from a very distant past, secure and inaccessible. The neurotic is repeating this past; his illness is an unfortunate variation on an old theme. The normal person, too—if there is such a person—is repeating this past; the neurotic only differs from him in that he got stuck in what the normal person succeeded (more or less) in conquering. These barriers, constructed in primeval times, provide the "meaning" of his and our existence.

JACQUES LACAN

The Deconstruction of the Drive

I ended my last talk by pointing out the place where I had taken you with the topological schematization of a certain division, and of a perimeter involuted upon itself, which is that constituted by what is usually called, quite incorrectly, the analytic situation.

This topology is intended to give you some notion of the location of the point of disjuncture and conjuncture, of union and frontier, that can be occupied only by the desire of the analyst.

To go further, to show you how this mapping is necessitated by all the deviations, of concept and of practice, that a long experience of analysis and of its doctrinal statements enables one to accumulate, I must—for those who have not been able, for purely practical reasons, to follow my earlier seminars—put forward the fourth concept that I have proposed as essential to the analytic experience—that of drive.

I

I can only write this introduction—this *Einführung*, to use Freud's term—in the wake of Freud, in so far as this notion is absolutely new in Freud.

The term *Trieb* certainly has a long history, not only in psychology or in physiology, but in physics itself and, of course, it is no accident that Freud chose this term. But he gave to *Trieb* so specific a use, and *Trieb* is so integrated into analytic practice itself, that its past is truly concealed. Just as the past of the term unconscious weights on the use of the term in analytic

Translated by Alan Sheridan. From *The Four Fundamental Concepts of Psychoanalysis*. Copyright © 1978 by W. W. Norton & Co.

theory—so, as far as *Trieb* is concerned, everyone uses it as a designation of a sort of radical given of our experience.

Sometimes, people even go so far as to invoke it against my doctrine of the unconscious, which they see as some kind of intellectualization—if they knew what I think of intelligence, they would certainly retract this criticism—as if I were ignoring what any analyst knows from experience, namely the domain of the drive. We will meet in experience something that has an irrepressible character even through repressions—indeed, if repression there must be, it is because there is something beyond that is pressing in. There is no need to go further in an adult analysis; one has only to be a child therapist to know the element that constitutes the clinical weight of each of the cases we have to deal with, namely, the drive. There seems to be here, therefore, a reference to some ultimate given, something archaic, primal. Such a recourse, which my teaching invites you to renounce if you are to understand the unconscious, seems inevitable here.

Now, is what we are dealing with in the drive essentially organic? Is it thus that we should interpret what Freud says in a text belonging to *Jenseits des Lustprinzips*—that the drive, *Trieb*, represents the *Ausserung der Trägheit*, some manifestation of inertia in the organic life? Is it a simple notion, which might be completed with reference to some storing away of this inertia, namely, to fixation, *Fixierung*?

Not only do I not think so, but I think that a serious examination of Freud's elaboration of the notion of drive runs counter to it.

Drive (*pulsion*) is not thrust (*poussée*). *Trieb* is not *Drang*, if only for the following reason. In an article written in 1915—that is, a year after the *Einführung zum Narzissmus*, you will see the importance of this reminder soon—entitled *Trieb und Triebschicksale*—one should avoid translating it by *avatar*, *Triebwandlungen* would be avatar, *Schicksal* is adventure, vicissitude—in this article, then, Freud says that it is important to distinguish four terms in the drive: *Drang*, thrust; *Quelle*, the source; *Objekt*, the object; *Ziel*, the aim. Of course, such a list may seem a quite natural one. My purpose is to prove to you that the whole text was written to show us that it is not as natural as that.

First of all, it is essential to remember that Freud himself tells us at the beginning of this article that the drive is a *Grundbegriff*, a fundamental concept. He adds, and in doing so shows himself to be a good epistemologist, that, from the moment when he, Freud, introduced the drive into science, one was faced with a choice between two possibilities—either this concept would be preserved, or it would be rejected. It would be preserved if it functioned, as one would now say—I would say if it traced its way in the real that it set out to penetrate. This is the case with all the other *Grundbegriffe* in the scientific domain.

What we see emerging here in Freud's mind are the fundamental concepts of physics. His masters in physiology are those who strive to bring to realization, for example, the integration of physiology with the fundamental concepts of modern physics, especially those connected with energy. How often, in the course of history, have the notions of energy and force been taken up and used again upon an increasingly totalized reality!

This is certainly what Freud foresaw. *The progress of knowledge*, he said, *can bear no* Starrheit, *no fascination with definitions*. Somewhere else, he says that the drive belongs to our myths. For my part, I will ignore this term myth—indeed, in the same text, in the first paragraph, Freud uses the word *Konvention*, convention, which is much closer to what we are talking about and to which I would apply the Benthamite term, *fiction*, which I have mapped for my followers. This term, I should say in passing, is much more preferable than that of *model*, which has been all too much abused. In any case, model is never a *Grundbegriff*, for, in a certan field, several models may function correlatively. This is not the case for a *Grundbegriff*, for a fundamental concept, nor for a fundamental fiction.

II

Now let us ask ourselves what appears first when we look more closely at the four terms laid down by Freud in relation to the drive. Let us say that these four terms cannot but appear disjointed.

First, *thrust* will be identified with a mere tendency to discharge. This tendency is what is produced by the fact of a stimulus, namely, the transmission of the accepted portion, at the level of the stimulus, of the additional energy, the celebrated Qn quantity of the *Entwurf*. But, on this matter, Freud makes, at the outset, a remark that has very far-reaching implications. Here, too, no doubt, there is stimulation, excitation, to use the term Freud uses at this level, *Reiz*, excitation. But the *Reiz* that is used when speaking of drive is different from any stimulation coming from the outside world, it is an internal *Reiz*. What does this mean?

In order to explicitate it, we have the notion of need, as it is manifested in the organism at several levels and first of all at the level of hunger and thirst. This is what Freud seems to mean when he distinguishes internal excitement from external excitement. Well! It has to be said that, at the very outset, Freud posits, quite categorically, that there is absolutely no question in *Trieb* of the pressure of a need such as *Hunger* or *Durst*, thirst.

What exactly does Freud mean by *Trieb*? Is he referring to something whose agency is exercised at the level of the organism in its totality? Does the real *qua* totality irrupt here? Are we concerned here with the living organism? No. It is always a question quite specifically of the Freudian field itself, in the most undifferentiated form that Freud gave it at the outset, which at this level, in the terms of the *Sketch* referred to above, that of the *Ich*, of the *Real-Ich*. The *Real-Ich* is conceived as supported, not by the organism as a whole, but by the nervous system. It has the character of a planned, objectified subject. I am stressing the surface characteristics of this field by treating it topologically, and in trying to show you how taking it in the form of a surface responds to all the needs of its handling.

This point is essential for, when we examine it more closely, we shall see that the *Triebreiz* is that by which certain elements of this field are, says Freud, *triebbesetzt*, invested as drive. This investment places us on the terrain of an energy—and not any energy—a potential energy, for—Freud articulated it in the most pressing way—the characteristic of the drive is to be a *konstante Kraft*, a constant force. He cannot conceive of it as a *momentane Stosskraft*.

What is meant by *momentane Stosskraft?* About this word *Moment*, we already have the example of a historical misunderstanding. During the siege of Paris in 1870, the Parisians made fun of Bismarck's *psychologische Moment*. This phrase struck them as being absurdly funny, for, until fairly recently, when they have had to get used to everything, the French have always been rather particular about the correct use of words. This quite new psychological moment struck them as being very funny indeed. All it meant was the psychological *factor*. But this *momentane Stosskraft* is not perhaps to be taken quite in the sense of factor, but rather in the sense of moment as used in the cinema. I think that this *Stosskraft*, or shock force, is simply a reference to the life force, to kinetic energy; it is not a question of something that will be regulated with movement. The discharge in question is of a quite different nature, and is on a quite different plane.

The constancy of the thrust forbids any assimilation of the drive to a biological function, which always has a rhythm. The first thing Freud says about the drive is, if I may put it this way, that it has no day or night, no spring or autumn, no rise and fall. It is a constant force. All the same, one must take account of the texts, and also of experience.

III

At the other end of the chain, Freud refers to *Befriedigung*, satisfaction, which he writes out in full, but in inverted commas. What does he mean by satisfaction of the drive? *Well, that's simple enough,* you'll say. *The satisfaction of the drive is reaching one's* Ziel, *one's aim.* The wild animal emerges from its hole *querens quem devoret,* and when he has found what he has to eat, he is satisfied, he digests it. The very fact that a similar image may be invoked shows that one allows it to resonate in harmony with mythology, with, strictly speaking, the drive.

One objection immediately springs to mind—it is rather odd that nobody should have noticed it, all the time it has been there, an enigma, which, like all Freud's enigmas, was sustained as a wager to the end of his life without Freud deigning to offer any further explanation—he probably left the work to those who could do it. You will remember that the third of the four fundamental vicissitudes of the drive that Freud posits at the outset—it is curious that there are *four* vicissitudes as there are *four* elements of the drive—is sublimation. Well, in this article, Freud tells us repeatedly that sublimation is also satisfaction of the drive, whereas it is *zielgehemmt*, inhibited as to its aim—it does not attain it. Sublimation is nonetheless satisfaction of the drive, without repression.

In other words—for the moment, I am not fucking, I am talking to you. Well! I can have exactly the same satisfaction as if I were fucking. That's what it means. Indeed, it raises the question of whether in fact I am not fucking at this moment. Between these two terms—drive and satisfaction—there is set up an extreme antinomy that reminds us that the use of the function of the drive has for me no other purpose than to put in question what is meant by satisfaction.

All those here who are psycho-analysts must now feel to what extent I am introducing here the most essential level of accommodation. It is clear that those with whom we deal, the patients, are not satisfied, as one says, with what they are. And yet, we know that everything they are, everything they experience, even their symptoms, involves satisfaction. They satisfy something that no doubt runs counter to that with which they might be satisfied, or rather, perhaps, they give satisfaction *to* something. They are not content with their state, but all the same, being in a state that gives so little content, they are content. The whole question boils down to the following—*what* is contented here?

On the whole, and as a first approximation, I would say that to which they give satisfaction by the ways of displeasure is nevertheless—and this is commonly accepted—the law of pleasure. Let us say that, for this sort of satisfaction, they give themselves too much trouble. Up to a point, it is this *too much trouble* that is the sole justification of our intervention.

One cannot say, then, that the aim is not attained where satisfaction is concerned. It is. This is not a definitive ethical position. But, at a certain level, this is how we analysts approach the problem—though we know a little more than others about what is normal and abnormal. We know that the forms of arrangement that exist between what works well and what works badly constitute a continuous series. What we have before us in analysis is a system in which everything turns out all right, and which attains its own sort of satisfaction. If we interfere in this, it is in so far as we think that there are other ways, shorter ones for example. In any case, if I refer to the drive, it is in so far as it is at the level of the drive that the state of satisfaction is to be rectified.

This satisfaction is paradoxical. When we look at it more closely, we see that something new comes into play—the category of the impossible. In the foundations of the Freudian conceptions, this category is an absolutely radical one. The path of the subject—to use the term in relation to which, alone, satisfaction may be situated—the path of the subject passes between the two walls of the impossible.

This function of the impossible is not to be approached without prudence, like any function that is presented in a negative form. I would simply like to suggest to you that the best way of approaching these notions is not to take them by negation. This method would bring us here to the question of the possible, and the impossible is not necessarily the contrary of the possible, or, since the opposite of the possible is certainly the real, we would be lead to define the real as the impossible.

Personally, I see nothing against this, especially as, in Freud, it is in this form that the real, namely, the obstacle to the pleasure principle, appears. The real is the impact with the obstacle; it is the fact that things do not turn out all right straight away, as the hand that is held out to external objects wishes. But I think this is a quite illusory and limited view of Freud's thought on this point. The real is distinguished, as I said last time, by its separation from the field of the pleasure principle, by its desexualization, by the fact that its economy, later, admits something new, which is precisely the impossible.

But the impossible is also present in the other field, as an essential element. The pleasure principle is even characterized by the fact that the impossible is so present in it that it is never recognized in it as such. The idea that the function of the pleasure principle is to satisfy itself by hallucination is there to illustrate this—it is only an illustration. By snatching at its object, the drive learns in a sense that this is precisely not the way it will be satisfied. For if one distinguishes, at the outset of the dialectic of the drive, *Not* from *Bedürfnis*, need from the pressure of the drive—it is precisely because no object of any *Not*, need, can satisfy the drive.

Even when you stuff the mouth—the mouth that opens in the register of the drive—it is not the food that satisfies it, it is, as one says, the pleasure of the mouth. That is why, in analytic experience, the oral drive is encountered at the final term, in a situation in which it does no more than order the menu. This is done no doubt with the mouth, which is fundamental to the satisfaction—what goes out from the mouth comes back to the mouth, and is exhausted in that pleasure that I have just called, by reference to the usual terms, the pleasure of the mouth.

This is what Freud tells us. Let us look at what he says—*As far as the object in the drive is concerned, let it be clear that it is, strictly speaking, of no importance. It is a matter of total indifference.* One must never read Freud without one's ears cocked. When one reads such things, one really ought to prick up one's ears.

How should one conceive of the object of the drive, so that one can say that, in the drive, whatever it may be, it is indifferent? As far as the oral drive is concerned, for example, it is obvious that it is not a question of food, nor of the memory of food, nor the echo of food, nor the mother's care, but of something that is called the breast, and which seems to go of its own accord because it belongs to the same series. If Freud makes a remark to the effect that the object in the drive is of no importance, it is probably because the breast, in its function as object, is to be revised in its entirety.

To this breast in its function as object, *objet a* cause of desire, in the sense that I understand the term—we must give a function that will explain its place in the satisfaction of the drive. The best formula seems to me to be the following—that *la pulsion en fait le tour.* I shall find other opportunities of applying it to other objects. *Tour* is to be understood here with the ambiguity it possesses in French, both *turn,* the limit around which one turns, and *trick.*

IV

I have left the question of the source till last. If we wished at all costs to introduce vital regulation into the function of the drive, one would certainly say that examining the source is the right way to go about it.

Why? Why are the so-called erogenous zones recognized only in those points that are differentiated for us by their rimlike structure? Why does one speak of the mouth and not of the oesophagus, or the stomach? They participate just as much in the oral function. But at the erogenous level we speak of the mouth, of the lips and the teeth, of what Homer calls the enclosure of the teeth.

The same goes for the anal drive. It is not enough to say that a certain vital function is integrated in a function of exchange with the world— excrement. There are other excremental functions, and there are other elements that participate in them other than the rim of the anus, which is however, specifically what, for us too, is defined as the source and departure of a certain drive.

Let me say that if there is anything resembling a drive it is a *montage.* It is not a *montage* conceived in a perspective referring to finality. This perspective is the one that is established in modern theories of instinct, in which the presentation of an image derived from *montage* is quite striking. Such a *montage*, for example, is the specific form that will make the hen in the farmyard run to ground if you place within a few yards of her the cardboard outline of a falcon, that is to say, something that sets off a more or less appropriate reaction, and where the trick is to show us that it is not necessarily an appropriate one. I am not speaking of this sort of *montage*.

The *montage* of the drive is a *montage* which, first, is presented as having neither head nor tail—in the sense in which one speaks of *montage* in a surrealist collage. If we bring together the paradoxes that we just defined at the level of *Drang*, at that of the object, at that of the aim of the drive, I think that the resulting image would show the working of a dynamo connected up to a gas-tap, a peacock's feather emerges, and tickles the belly of a pretty woman, who is just lying there looking beautiful. Indeed, the thing begins to become interesting from this very fact, that the drive defines, according to Freud, all the forms of which one may reverse such a mechanism. This does not mean that one turns the dynamo upside-down—one unrolls its wires, it is they that become the peacock's feather, the gas-tap goes into the lady's mouth, and the bird's rump emerges in the middle.

This is what he shows as a developed example. Read this text of Freud's between now and next time, and you will see that it constantly jumps, without transition, between the most heterogeneous images. All this occurs only by means of grammatical references, the artifice of which you will find easy to grasp next time.

Incidentally, how can one say, just like that, as Freud goes on to do, that exhibitionism is the contrary of voyeurism, or that masochism is the contrary of sadism? He posits this simply for grammatical reasons, for reasons concerning the inversion of the subject and the object, as if the grammatical object and subject were real functions. It is easy to show that this is not the case, and we have only to refer to our structure of our language for this deduction to become impossible. But what, by means of this game, he conveys to us about the essence of the drive is what, next time, I will define for you as the trace of the act.

PAUL RICOEUR

Religion and Fantasy

The question of the nonregressive, nonarchaizing sources of religion leads to a critical examination of the representational nucleus that Freud thinks he has delimited by the convergent paths of clinical description and ethnology: the fantasy of the killing of the father. For Freud, the return of the repressed is both the return of the affects of fear and love, anxiety and consolation, and the return of the fantasy itself in the substitute figure of god. This substitute figure is the remote derivative of the representations attaching to the instinctual substrate. Consequently, all our remarks about a possible epigenesis of religious feeling become meaningful only through the mediation of an epigenesis at the level of representations.

This epigenesis, however, is simply ruled out in Freudianism because of the status accorded to the fantasy of the murder of the primal father. An essential element of the Freudian interpretation is that this murder actually occurred in the past either once or several times, and that there exists an actual memory of it inscribed in the hereditary patrimony of mankind. The Oedipus complex of the individual is too brief and too indistinct to engender the gods; without an ancestral crime as part of our phylogenetic past, the longing for the father is unintelligible; *the* father is not *my* father. Through the course of the years, Freud kept reinforcing the notion that the memory of the primal killing is a memory of a real event. The most explicit statements in this regard are those in *Moses and Monotheism*, which we have cited at length in the "Analytic." If then, for Freud, religion is archaic and repetitive, it is to a great extent because religion is drawn backward by the remembrance of a

Translated by Denis Savage. From *Freud and Philosophy: An Essay on Interpretation.* Copyright © 1970 by Yale University Press.

murder that belongs to its prehistory and constitutes what *Moses and Monotheism* calls "the truth in religion." The truth resides in memory: whatever is added by the imagination is, as in dreams, distortion; whatever is added by rational thought is, again as in dreams, secondary elaboration, rationalization, and superstition. Thus Freud deliberately turns his back on the demythologizing interpretations which, from Schelling to Bultmann, deprive myths of any etiological function so as to restore to them their mytho-poetic function capable of leading to a reflection or a speculation.

It is strange to note that in order to explain religion Freud held onto a conception he was forced to abandon in the theory of the neuroses. We recall that the true interpretation of the Oedipus complex was achieved in opposition to the erroneous theory of the real seduction of the child by an adult. Unfortunately, the Oedipus episode, which Freud discovered by a sort of reversal of meaning of the seduction scene, was substituted in its place; the Oedipus complex was made the trace or vestige of a real memory (this vestigial function, we recall, is what enabled Freud in Chapter 7 of *The Interpretation of Dreams* to equate formal regression with the quasi-hallucinatory revival of a memory trace). Even more than the individual Oedipus complex, the collective complex of mankind is regarded as the return of a vestigial type of affect and representation.

Freud himself, however, furnishes the means of picturing the matter in another way. There is in Freud a conception of the "primal scene" in which the notion of a nonvestigial function of imagination is sketched. The "scene with the vulture," Freud notes in the *Leonardo*, "would not be a memory of Leonardo's but a fantasy, which he formed at a later date and transposed to his childhood." Freud illustrates this by a comparison with the way in which the writing of history might have originated among the peoples of antiquity, when men entered an "age of reflection" and

> felt a need to learn where they had come from and how they had developed. . . . Historical writing, which had begun to keep a continuous record of the present, now also cast a glance back to the past, gathered traditions and legends, interpreted the traces of antiquity that survived in customs and usages, and in this way created a history of the past.

This "history of a nation's earliest days, which was compiled later and for tendentious reasons"—does it not imply a *creation of meaning*, capable of marking off and carrying what we have called an epigenesis of religious feeling? May not such a primal scene fantasy supply the first layer of meaning to an imagination of origins which is increasingly detached from its function of infantile and quasi-neurotic repetition, and increasingly of service to an investigation of the fundamental meanings of human destiny?

Freud encountered this nonvestigial product of imagination, this carrier of a new meaning, not when he spoke of religion but when he spoke of art. Let us recall our exegesis of the Gioconda's smile. The memory of the lost mother, we said, is recreated by the work of art; it is not something that lies hidden underneath, like a real stratum that is merely covered over; strictly speaking, it is a creation, and exists only insofar as it is presented in the painting.

Hence one and the same fantasy can carry two opposed vectors: a regressive vector which subjects the fantasy to the past, and a progressive vector which makes it an indicator of meaning. That the regressive and progressive functions can coexist in the same fantasy is intelligible in Freudian terms. Leonardo's vulture fantasy is a first transfiguration of the vestiges of the past; a fortiori, a true work of art like the Gioconda is a creation in which, in Freud's own words, the past is "denied and overcome."

Freud admits, however, that he does not understand this creative function: "Since artistic talent and capacity are intimately connected with sublimation we must admit that the nature of the artistic function is also inaccessible to us along psycholanalytic lines."

Let us apply this remark to the fantasy of the primal crime. Freud writes in the *Leonardo*:

> Psychoanalysis has made us familiar with the intimate connection between the father complex and belief in God; it has shown us that a personal God is, psychologically, nothing other than an exalted father. . . . The almighty and just God, and kindly Nature, appear to us as grand sublimations of father and mother, or rather as revivals and restorations of the young child's ideas of them.

Why should not this sublimation of the father involve the same ambiguity, the same double value of oneiric revival and cultural creation? Such must be the case, in a certain sense, even within the framework of Freud's interpretation, if religion is to fulfill its universal and not just its individual function—if it is to acquire cultural importance and assume a function of protection, consolation, reconciliation. But then is it possible that the father figure, as presented by religion and faith, is merely a picture puzzle, hidden in the believer's invocation like Leonardo's vulture in the folds of the Virgin's robe? To my mind one cannot treat the father figure as an isolated figure with its own special exegesis; it is simply one component—the central one, it is true, as we shall say further on—in a mytho-poetic constellation which must first be considered as a whole.

Let us explore the following path. The force of a religious symbol lies in the fact that it recaptures a primal scene fantasy and transforms it into an instrument of discovery and exploration of origins. Through these "detector" representations, man tells the origin of his humanity. Thus the accounts of battle in Hesiod and the Babylonian literature, the accounts of fall in the Orphic literature, the accounts of primal guilt and exile in the Hebraic literature, may indeed be treated, in the manner of Otto Rank, as a sort of collective oneirism, but this oneirism is not a recording of prehistory. Rather, through their vestigial function, such symbols show in operation an imagination of origins, which may be said to be historical, *geschichtlich,* for it tells of an advent, a coming to being, but not historical, *historisch,* for it has no chronological significance. To use Husserlian terminology, I will say that the fantasies explored by Freud make up the hyletic of this mytho-poetic imagination. It is in and through certain primal scene fantasies that man "forms," "interprets," "intends" meanings of another order, meanings capable of becoming the signs of the sacred which the philosophy of reflection can only acknowledge and salute at the horizon of its archeology and its teleology. This new intentionality, through which fantasies are interpreted symbolically, arises from the very nature of the fantasies insofar as they speak of the lost origin, of the lost archaic object, of the lack inherent in desire; what gives rise to the endless movement of the interpretation is not the fullness of memory but its emptiness, its openness. Ethnology, comparative mythology, biblical exegesis—all confirm that every myth is a reinterpretation of an earlier account. These interpretations of interpretations are quite capable therefore of operating upon fantasies pertaining to various ages and stages of the libido. But the important factor is not so much this "sensory matter" as the movement of interpretation that is contained in the advancement of meaning and constitutes the intentional transforming of the "matter." This is the reason why a *hermêneutikê technê* can be applied to myths; a myth is already *hermêneia,* interpretation and reinterpreation of its own roots. And if myths assume a theological meaning, as we see in the origin narratives, they do so through this endless process of correction, which has become a concerted and systematic effort.

Thus the father figure cannot be considered apart from the mytho-poetic function in which it is inserted. It is true that this figure is particularly dominant, since it furnishes the prototype of the deity and thus refers, through polytheism and then monotheism, to the unique father figure. This "projective" characteristic is found only in the father figure; that is true. But Freud did not struggle with the difficulties concerning projection as he did with those concerning introjection and identification. The displacement of the father onto the totem animal and the totem god does not perplex him enough. The analogy with animal phobias and with paranoia dispense him from seeking further. Do not the same questions that we asked concerning the mother image in Leonardo's Mona Lisa arise here? Is not the father figure as much "denied and overcome" as it is "repeated"? What have I understood when I have discovered—or divined—the father figure in the representation of the deity? Do I understand both of them better? But I do not know what the father means. The primal scene fantasy refers me back to an unreal father, a father who is missing from our individual and collective history; this is the fantasy in which I imagine God as a father. So great is my ignorance of the father that I can say that the father as a cultural theme is created by mythology on the basis of an oneiric fantasy. I did not know what the father was until his image had engendered the whole series of his derivatives. What constitutes the father as an origin myth is the interpretation through which the primal scene fantasy receives a new intention—to the point where I can invoke "our Father, who art in heaven . . ." Stated in the prephilosophical language of myth, the symbolism of the heavens and the symbolism of the father make explicit the origin symbolism that the archaic fantasy virtually contained by reason of absence, lack, loss, and emptiness of its proper "object."

Why does the father figure have a privilege that the mother figure does not have? Its privileged status is no doubt due to its extremely rich symbolic power, in particular its potential for "transcendence." In symbolism, the father figures less as a begetter equal to the mother than as the name-giver and the lawgiver. Freud's remarks about identification with a model, as distinct from libidinal identification, are applicable here. One does not possess the father of identification, not only because he is a lost archaic object, but because he is distinct from every archaic object. As such, he cannot "come back" or "return" except as a cultural theme; the father of identification is a task for representation because from the start he is not an object of desire but the source of institution. The father is an unreality set apart, who, from the start, is a being of language. Because he is the name-giver, he is the name-problem, as the Hebrews first conceived him. Thus the father figure was bound to have a richer and more articulated destiny than the mother figure. Through sublimation and identification the symbol of the father was able to join with that of the lord and that of the heavens to form the symbolism of an ordered, wise, and just transcendence, as outlined by Mircea Eliade in the first chapter of his *Histoire comparée des religions*.

But then the father figure is not simply a return of the repressed; it is rather the result of a true process of creation. This creation of meaning constitutes the true overdetermination of authentic symbols, and this overdetermination in turn grounds the possibility of two hermeneutics, one of which unmasks the archaism of its fantasy content, while the other discovers the new intention that animates the material content. The reconciliation of the two hermeneutics lies in symbols themselves. Thus one cannot stop with an antithetic that would distinguish between "two sources of morality and religion" for the prophecy of consciousness is not external to its archeology.

One might even say that, thanks to their overdetermined structure, symbols succeed in inverting the temporal signs of the origin fantasy. The primal father signifies the eschaton, the "God who comes"; generation signifies regeneration; birth analogously stands for rebirth; the childhood— that childhood which is behind me—signifies the other childhood, the "second naïveté." The process of becoming conscious is ultimately a process of seeing one's childhood in front of oneself and one's death behind oneself: "before, you were dead . . ."; "unless you become as little children . . ." In this interchange of birth and death, the symbolism of the God who comes has taken over and justified the figure of the primal father.

But if symbols are fantasies that have been denied and overcome, they are never fantasies that have been abolished. That is why one is never certain that a given symbol of the sacred is not simply a "return of the repressed"; or rather, it is always certain that each symbol of the sacred is also and at the same time a revival of an infantile and archaic symbol. The two functions of symbol remain inseparable. The symbolic meanings closest to theological and philosophical speculation are always involved with some trace of an archaic myth. This close alliance of archaism and prophecy constitutes the richness of religious symbolism; it also constitutes its ambiguity. "Symbols give rise to thought," but they are also the birth of idols. That is why the critique of idols remains the condition of the conquest of symbols.

It seems to me that the two preceding discussions lead to a third sphere of problems. After seeing the projected shadow or imprint of the advancement of meaning in instincts and fantasies, we must consider speech or the spoken word [la parole], for this is the element in which the advancement of meaning occurs. If an epigenesis of instincts and fantasies is possible, it is because speech is the instrument of the hermêneia or "interpretation" that symbols exercise with respect to fantasies, even before symbols are themselves interpreted by the exegetes.

The ascending dialectic of affect and fantasy is thus carried by an ascending dialectic of symbolic language. But this creation of meaning implies that the imaginary of the mytho-poetic function is more closely related to nascent speech than to images in the sense of a mere revival of perception. Unfortunately, the Freudian conception of language is very inadequate; the meaning of words is the revival of acoustic images; thus language itself is a "trace" of perception. This vestigial conception of language can give no support to an epigenesis of meaning. If it is true that the various degrees of fantasy are developed only in the element of language, it is still necessary to distinguish between "things heard" and "things seen." But things heard are first of all things said; and things said, in myths of the origin and the end, are the exact contrary of traces or vestiges. The things said interpret certain primal scene fantasies in order to *speak* of man's situation in the sacred.

The inadequacy of Freud's philosophy of language explains, I believe, what seems to me to be Freud's greatest shortcoming in his theory of religion: he thought he could make a direct psychology of the superego and, on this basis, a direct psychology of belief and the believer, thus circumventing an exegesis of the *texts* in and through which the religious man has "formed" and "educated" his belief, in the sense of the *Bildung* mentioned above. However, it is impossible to construct a psychoanalysis of belief apart from an interpretation and understanding of the cultural productions in which the object of belief announces itself.

What we have said in general about the process of man's "becoming conscious" should be said more specifically about his "becoming religious." For man, to become conscious is to be drawn away from his archaism by the series of figures that institute and constitute him as man. Hence there can be no question of grasping the meaning of the religious man apart from the meaning of the texts that are the documents of his belief. Dilthey very clearly established this point in his famous essay of 1900, "Die Entstehung der Hermeneutik." Understanding or interpretation, he says, does not truly begin until "life-expressions" are fixed in an objectivity that is subject to the technical rules of an art: "We call this technical understanding of durably fixed life-expressions an exegesis or interpretation." If literature is the privileged area of this process of interpretation—though one may also legitimately speak of a hermeneutics of sculpture and of painting—it is because language is the only complete, exhaustive, and objectively intelligible expression of human interiority: "That is why," Dilthey continues, "the art of understanding centers around the exegesis or interpretation of the written testimony of human existence."

There is hardly any need to state that *Moses and Monotheism* does not operate at the level of an exegesis of the Old Testament and in no way satisfies the most elementary requirements of a hermeneutics adapted to a text. Consequently one cannot say that Freud truly made, or even began to make, an "analysis of religious representations," whereas on the esthetic plane the "Moses" of Michelangelo is truly treated as a self-contained work and analyzed in detail, with no concession made to a direct psychology of the artist and his creative activity. The works of religion, the monuments of belief, are treated neither with the same sympathy nor with the same rigor; instead, we are presented with a vague relationship between religious themes and the paternal prototype. Freud has decided once and for all that the truly religious ideas are those that clearly stem from this prototype. A powerful being who rules over nature as an empire, who annuls death and redresses the afflictions of this life—if God is to be God, this is all he can be; naïve religion is religion proper. Philosophic religion and "oceanic" religion, in which the personality of God has been softened, transposed, or abandoned, are derivatives or secondary rationalizations that refer back to the paternal prototype.

I would like to show, in the case of two particular themes central to the Freudian problematic—the themes of guilt and consolation—how a path that Freud has closed may be reopened.

The first theme has to do with religion as the summit of an ethical view of the world; the second concerns religion as proceeding from a suspension of the ethical. These themes are the two focal points of religious consciousness, as Freud himself acknowledges by viewing religion as a form of interdiction and as a form of consolation.

Now, Freud had no interest whatsoever in what might be called an epigenesis of the sense of guilt, an epigenesis that would be guided by an increasingly refined symbolism. The sense of guilt seems to have no history beyond the Oedipus complex and its dissolution. It remains a preventive procedure with respect to anticipated punishment. In the Freudian literature, the sense of guilt is consistently understood in this archaic sense. But an epigenesis of guilt cannot be directly established by a psychology of the superego; it can only be deciphered by the indirect means of a textual exegesis of the penitential literature. In this literature there is constituted an exemplary history of conscience (Gewissen). Man arrives at adult, normal, ethical guilt when he understands himself *according to* the figures of this exemplary history. Elsewhere I have tried to investigate the notions of stain, sin, and guilt by means of an exegesis in Dilthey's sense of the term. I found that guilt progresses by crossing two thresholds. The first threshold is that of injustice— in the sense of the Jewish prophets and also of Plato. The fear of being unjust, the remorse for having been unjust, are no longer taboo fears; damage to the interpersonal relationship, wrongs done to the person of another, treated as a means and not as an end, mean more than a feeling of a threat of castration. Thus the consciousness of injustice marks a creation of meaning by comparison with the fear of vengeance, the fear of being punished. The second threshold is that of the sin of the just man, of the evil of justice proper; here consciousness discovers the radical evil affecting every maxim, even that of the good man.

All we have said above concerning the function of fantasies is relevant here. The myths in which the advance of consciousness is expressed are certainly built upon primal scene fantasies subject to the anxiety of the superego. That is why guilt is a trap, an occasion of backwardness, of fixation in premorality, of stagnation in archaism. But the mythic intentionality resides in the series of interpretations and reinterpretations through which a myth rectifies its own archaic substrate. Thus are constituted the symbols of evil which invite thought and upon which I can form the notion of bad or servile will. Between the sense of guilt in the psychoanalytic sense and radical evil in the Kantian sense there extends a series of figures in which each figure takes up the preceding one to "deny" and "overcome" it, as Freud says of the work of art. It would be the task of reflective thought to show how this progressive consciousness follows the progression of the symbolic spheres we sketched in the first part of this chapter. The same figures that served to mark off the path of feeling—the figures of possession, domination, and valuation—are also the successive regions of our alienation. This is understandable, for if these figures are the symbols of our fallibility, they are also the symbols of our having already fallen. Freedom becomes alienated in alienating its own mediations, economic, political, cultural. The servile will, one might add, mediates itself by passing through all the figures of our helplessness that express and objectify our power of existing.

This indirect method could be the means of elaborating the notion of noninfantile, nonarchaic, non-neurotic sources of our guilt. But just as desire intrudes into these successive spheres and mixes its ramifications with the nonerotic functions of the self, so too the affective archaism of guilt extends into all the regions of alienated possession, of unmeasured power, of vainglorious pretensions of worth. That is why guilt remains ambiguous and suspect. In order to break its false prestige, we must always focus on it the double illumination of a demystifying interpretation that denounces its archaism and a restorative interpretation that places the birth of evil in the mind or spirit itself.

I have taken the example of guilt as the prime example of an ambiguous notion, both archaic in origin and susceptible of an indefinite creation of meaning. This same ambiguity is written into the heart of religion, insofar as the symbols of salvation are on the same level and of the same quality as the symbols of evil. It can be shown that for all the figures of accusation there are corresponding figures of redemption. As a result, the central figure of religion, which psychoanalysis tells us proceeds from the prototype of the father, cannot complete its own genesis until it has traversed all the degrees corresponding to those of guilt. Thus the interpretation of the father fantasy in the symbolism of God extends into all the regions of accusation and redemption.

But if the symbolic representation of God progresses in parallel with the symbols of evil and guilt, it is not completed within this correlation. As Freud well saw, religion is more an art of bearing the hardships of life than an indefinite exorcism of the paternal accusation. This cultural function of consolation is what places religion no longer merely in the sphere of fear, but in that of desire. Plato already said in the *Phaedo* that there remains in each of us an infant to be consoled. The question is whether the function of consolation is merely infantile, or whether there is not also what I should now call an epigenesis or ascending dialectic of consolation.

Once again literature is the medium that marks off the progress of this rectification of consolation. The objection may be made that the critique of the old law of retribution, a critique already made by the wise men of Babylon and even more by the books of the Hebrews, is not a part of religion. But then we must enter into another problematic, which Freudianism seems to be ignorant of, the problematic of the internal conflict between faith and religion: it is the faith of Job and not the religion of his friends that should be confronted with the Freudian iconoclasm. Does not this faith accomplish part of the task Freud assigns to whoever undertakes to "do without his father" (*Leonardo*)? Job receives no explanation of his suffering; he is merely shown something of the grandeur and order of the whole, without any meaning being directly given to the finite point of view of his desire. His faith is closer to the "third kind" of knowledge in Spinoza's sense than to any religion of Providence. A path is thus opened, a path of non-narcissistic reconciliation: I give up my point of view; I love the whole; I make ready to say: "The intellectual love of the mind toward God is a part of that very love of God whereby God loves himself" (*quo Deus seipsum amat*). Through the twofold test of commandment and retribution, faith brings about a single and unique suspension of the ethical. By revealing the sin of the just man, the man of belief goes beyond the ethics of righteousness; by losing the immediate consolation of his narcissism, he goes beyond any ethical view of the world.

Through this twofold test he overcomes the father figure; but in losing it as an idol he perhaps discovers it as a symbol. The father symbol is the surplus of meaning intended by the *seipsum* of the Spinozist theorem. The father symbol is not a symbol of a father whom I can have; in this respect the father is nonfather. Rather, the father symbol is the likeness of the father in accordance with which the giving up of desire is no longer death but love, in the sense once more of the corollary of the Spinozist theorem: "The love of God toward men and the intellectual love of the mind toward God are one and the same thing."

We have reached a point here that seems unsurpassable. It is not a point of repose but of tension, for it is not yet apparent how the "personality" of God who pardons and the "impersonality" of *Deus sive natura* could coincide. I only say that the two ways of suspending the ethical, Kierkegaard's and Spinoza's, may be the same, as we are led to think by the *Deus seipsum amat* of Spinoza and by the dialectic, underlying the whole of Western theology, of "God" and "deity"; but I do not know they are the same.

Starting from this extreme point, a final confrontation with Freud may be proposed. To the very end we must refuse having to choose between two platitudes: that of the apologist, who would completely reject the Freudian iconoclasm, and that of the eclectic, who would juxtapose the iconoclasm of religion and the symbolism of faith. For my part I will apply, as a last and ultimate resort, the dialectic of the *yes* and the *no* to the principle of reality. Ultimately, this is the level on which the "epigenesis of consolation" according to faith and the "resignation to Ananke" according to Freudianism confront and challenge one another.

I make no secret of the fact that the reading of Freud is what has helped me extend the critique of narcissism—which I have constantly called the false Cogito, or the abortive Cogito—to its most extreme consequences regarding the religious desire for consolation; the reading of Freud is what helped me place the "giving up of the father" at the heart of the problematic of faith. In return I do not conceal my dissatisfaction with the Freudian interpretation of the reality principle. Freud's scientism prevented him from following to completion a certain path glimpsed in the *Leonardo*, even though this was the harshest book Freud wrote against religion.

As we have said, reality is not simply a set of observable facts and verifiable laws; reality is also, in psychoanalytic terms, the world of things and of men, such as that world would appear to a human desire which has given up the pleasure principle, that is to say, which has subordinated its point of view to the whole. But then, I asked, is reality merely Ananke? Is reality simply necessity offered to my resignation? Is it not also possibility opened to the power of loving? This question I decipher at my own risk—through the questions Freud himself raises concerning the destiny of Leonardo: "Quite apart from doubts about a possible transformation of the instinct to investigate back into an enjoyment of life—a transformation which we must take as fundamental in the tragedy of Faust—the view may be hazarded that Leonardo's development approaches Spinoza's mode of thinking." And further on:

> Lost in admiration and filled with true humility, he all too easily forgets that he himself is a part of those active forces and that in accordance with the scale of his personal strength the way is open for him to try to alter a small portion of the destined course of the world—a world in which the small is still no less wonderful and significant than the great.

And what can be the meaning of the last lines of the *Leonardo?*

> We all still show too little respect for Nature which (in the obscure words of Leonardo which recall Hamlet's lines) "is full of countless reasons that

never enter experience." [*La natura è piena d'infinite ragioni che non furono mai in isperienza.*] Every one of us human beings corresponds to one of the countless experiments in which these "*ragioni*" of nature force their way into experience.

I see in these lines a quiet invitation to identify reality with nature and nature with Eros. These "active forces," these "countless reasons that never enter experience," these "countless experiments" in which those reasons "force their way into experience"—these are not observed facts, but rather powers, the diversified power of nature and life. But I cannot apprehend this power except in a mythical symbolism of creation. Is this not the reason why the destroyers of images, ideals, and idols end by mythicizing reality in opposition to illusion—describing illusion as Dionysus, innocence of becoming, eternal return, and reality as Ananke, Logos? Is not this remythicizing a sign that the discipline of reality is nothing without the grace of imagination? that the consideration of necessity is nothing without the evocation of possibility? Through these questions the Freudian hermeneutics can be related to another hermeneutics, a hermeneutics that deals with the mytho-poetic function and regards myths not as fables, i.e. stories that are false, unreal, illusory, but rather as the symbolic exploration of our relationship to beings and to Being. What carries this mytho-poetic function is another power of language, a power that is no longer the demand of desire, demand for protection, demand for providence, but a call in which I leave off all demands and listen.

Thus do I attempt to construct the *yes* and the *no* which I pronounce about the psychoanalysis of religion. The faith of the believer cannot emerge intact from this confrontation, but neither can the Freudian conception of reality. To the cleavage the *yes* to Freud introduces into the heart of the faith of believers, separating idols from symbols, there corresponds the cleavage the *no* to Freud introduces into the heart of the Freudian reality principle, separating mere resignation to Ananke from the love of Creation.

RICHARD WOLLHEIM

Freud and the Understanding of Art

F reud opens his ingenious and revealing essay on the *Moses* of Michelangelo with a disclaimer. He had, he said, no more than a layman's or amateur's knowledge of art: neither in his attitude to art nor in the way in which he experienced its attractions was he a connoisseur. He goes on:

> Nevertheless, works of art do exercise a powerful effect on me, especially those of literature and sculpture, less often of painting. This has occasioned me, when I have been contemplating such things, to spend a long time before them trying to apprehend them in my own way, i.e. to explain to myself what their effect is due to. Wherever I cannot do this, as for instance with music, I am almost incapable of obtaining any pleasure. Some rationalistic, or perhaps analytic, turn of mind in me rebels against being moved by a thing without knowing why I am thus affected and what it is that affects me.

And then, as if for a moment conscious that he might appear to be imposing his own personal peculiarities, a quirk of his own temperament, upon a subject with its own code, with its own imperatives, he hastens to concede what he calls "the apparently paradoxical fact" that "precisely some of the grandest and most overwhelming creations of art are still unsolved riddles to our understanding." Before these works we feel admiration, awe—and bewilderment. "Possibly," Freud goes on with that irony which he permitted himself in talking of established ways of thinking

> some writer on aesthetics has discovered that this state of intellectual bewilderment is a necessary condition when a work of art is to achieve its greatest effects. It would be only with the greatest reluctance that I could bring myself to believe in any such necessity.

Anyone acquainted with Freud's style will at once recognize something typical in this whole passage, in the easy and informal way with which from the beginning he takes the reader into his confidence: typical, too, that Freud should be unable to renounce this natural way of writing even when, as here, the work on which he was engaged was ultimately to appear anonymously.

Nevertheless, for all its ease of manner, the passage that I have quoted is problematic. These are two questions to which it immediately gives rise, and to which some kind of answer is required, if we are to use it as providing us with an entry into Freud's views about art. The first is this: When Freud says that for him there is a peculiar difficulty in obtaining pleasure from a work of art if he cannot explain to himself the source of this pleasure, are we to take his words—as he says he wants us to—as a purely personal avowal? Or is it that what constituted for Freud the peculiarity of his situation is simply the deeper understanding he feels himself to have of human nature and human achievement: that the attitude to art from which he cannot free himself is one that must come naturally to anyone affected by psychoanalysis, and that it is only in ignorance of psychoanalysis that any other attitude—for instance, that of delight in bewilderment—could be conceived? And the second question is, What form of understanding or explanation did Freud have in mind? More specifically, we know that by 1913, the date of the Michelangelo essay, Freud had already subjected a large number of psychic phenomena, normal as well as pathological, to psychoanalytic scrutiny: dreams, errors, jokes, symptoms, the psychoneuroses themselves, phantasies, magic. And so it is only natural to ask which of these phenomena, if any, was to serve as the model, so far as the pattern of explanation it received, for the understanding of art?

The first question is one that I shall return to later. Meanwhile I should like to draw your attention to a passage from another and certainly no less famous essay that Freud wrote on a great artist, "A Childhood Memory of Leonardo da Vinci," which dates from the spring of 1910. Writing of Leonardo's insatiable curiosity, Freud quotes two sayings of Leonardo's, both to the effect that one cannot love or hate in any but a faint or feeble way unless one has a thorough knowledge of the object of one's love or hate. Freud then goes on:

> The value of these remarks of Leonardo's is not to be looked for in their conveying an important psychological fact; for what they assert is obviously false, and Leonardo must have known this as well as we do. It is not true that human beings delay loving or hating until they have studied and become familiar with the nature of the object to which these affects apply. On the contrary they love impulsively, from emotional motives which have nothing to do with knowledge, and whose operation is at most weakened by reflection and consideration. Leonardo, then, could only have meant that the love practised by human beings was not of the proper and unobjectionable kind: one *should* love in such a way as to hold back the affect, subject it

to the process of reflection and only let it take its course when it has stood up to the test of thought. And at the same time we understand that he wishes to tell us that it happens so in his case and that it would be worth while for everyone else to treat love and hatred as he does.

Now, it must be emphasized that the two sayings of Leonardo with which Freud takes issue do not refer simply to personal loves and hates: they are addressed to what we feel about anything in nature. Indeed, in the longer of the two passages that Freud cites Leonardo is—or at any rate Freud takes him to be—expressly defending himself against the charge that a scientific attitude towards the works of creation evinces coldness or irreligion. If, then, Leonardo's attitude, so understood, is thought by Freud to deserve these strictures, it is worth setting them by the side of Freud's own attitude to art, as we so far have it, and wondering why they do not apply to it.

Turning now to the second of the two questions, I shall anticipate the course of this lecture to the extent of saying that Freud seems to find in a variety of mental phenomena suitable models for the interpretation of art: that in attempting to explain art he assimilates it now to this, now to that, psychic phenomenon, for the understanding of which he had already devised its own explanatory schema. The richness of Freud's aesthetic lies in the overlapping of these various suggestions: though, as we shall see, how the suggestions are actually to be fitted together is an issue to which Freud barely applied himself.

However, before either of the two questions that arise out of the Michelangelo essay can be answered, there is a third which requires our attention. And that is the question of what texts we are to consult, and what relative assessment we are to make of them, in arriving at a considered estimate of Freud's views. In addition to its obvious priority, this question has the additional advantage that, if taken early on, it might save us time later. For a mere review of Freud's writings on art and of their relative weight could show us where his central interests lay: it could show us the kind or kinds of understanding he sought and the significance that he attached to this. It could save us from certain mistakes.

For the first thing to be observed about Freud's writings on art is that some of them are only peripherally about art. A fact that emerges from Ernest Jones's biography is that Freud, for all his lack of arrogance, felt himself, in a way that is perhaps vanishing from the world, to be one of the great, to belong in a pantheon of the human race: and for this reason it was only natural that his thoughts should often turn to the great figures of the past, and that to understand the inner workings of their genius should be one of his recurrent ambitions. Freud, we may think, wrote *about* Leonardo in much the same spirit as later, at one of the dark moments of European civilization, he was to write *to* Einstein: it was the conscious communion of one great man with another.

My claim is, then, that the essay on Leonardo—and much the same sort of claim could be mounted for the essay on Dostoevsky—is primarily a study in psychoanalytic biography: and the connection with art is *almost* exhausted by the fact that the subject of the biography happens to be one of the greatest, as well as one of the strangest, artists in history. For if we turn to the text of the essay, and ignore the straightforward contributions to psycho-analytic theory, which are inserted, as it were, parenthetically, we shall see that the study falls into two parts.

There is, first of all, the reconstruction of Leonardo's childhood, the evidence for which is recognized to be scanty: and then there is the history of Leonardo's adult life, which is, of course, adequately documented, but which is deliberately presented by Freud in such a way that it can be connected up with earlier events. In other words, seen as a whole, the essay is an attempt to exhibit—not, of course, to prove but, like the clinical case-histories, to exhibit—the dependence of adult capacities and proclivities on the infantile, and in particular on infantile sexuality.

More specifically, the dependence of later on earlier experience is worked out in terms of fixation points and successive regressions. To Leo-nardo are attributed two fixation points. The first or earlier one was es-tablished in the years spent in his mother's house when, experiencing as an illegitimate child her undivided love, he was seduced into a sexual precocity in which intensive sexual curiosity and an element of sadism must have been manifestations. In time, however, a conjunction of internal and external factors—the very excess of the boy's love for his mother, and his reception into the nobler household of his father and his step-mother by his fifth year—brought on a wave of repression in which the blissful eroticism of his infancy was stamped out. He overcame and yet preserved his feelings for his mother by first identifying himself with her and then seeking as sexual objects not other women but boys in his own likeness. Here we have Leonardo's second point of fixation, in an idealized homosexuality: idealized, for he loves boys only as his mother loved him: that is, in a sublimated fashion.

It is against this childhood background that Freud then reviews and interprets the successive phases of Leonardo's adult life. First, there was a phase in which he worked without inhibition. Then, gradually his powers of decision began to fail, and his creativity became enfeebled under the inroads of an excessive and brooding curiosity. Finally, there was a phase in which his gifts reasserted themselves in a series of works that have become justly famous for their enigmatic quality. These last two phases Freud then proceeds to connect with successive regressions, in the manner that had become familiar since the *Three Essays on the Theory of Sexuality*. First, there is a regression to a strong but totally repressed homosexuality, in which the greater part of the libido, profiting from pathways laid down in a yet earlier phase, seeks and finds an outlet in the pursuit of knowledge—though, as we have seen, at a heavy cost to the general conduct of life. This, however, is then overtaken by a regression to the earliest attachment. Either through some internal transformations of energy or by a happy accident—Freud suggests a connection with the sitter for the *Mona Lisa*—Leonardo, now at the age of fifty, returns to enjoy his mother's love in a way that allows a new release of creativity.

Now it is in connection with this attempt to interpret Leonardo's adult life in the light of certain childhood patterns that Freud appeals to particular works of Leonardo all drawn from the later phase: the *Mona Lisa*, the Paris and London versions of the *Madonna and Child with St Anne*, and the late androgynous figure paintings. If we read the relevant section of Freud's essay (section IV) carefully, we see what his procedure is. He uses the evidence provided by the pictures to confirm the link he has postulated between this last phase of Leonardo's activity and a certain infantile "complex," as Freud would have put it at that date. Note that Freud does not use the evidence of the pictures to establish the infantile complex—that depends upon secondary sources and the so-called "infantile memory" from which the essay derives its title: he uses it to establish a link between the complex and something else. But, we might ask: In what way do the pictures that Freud cites provide evidence? And the answer is that the evidence that they provide comes from certain internal features plus certain obvious or seemingly obvious trains of association to these features. So in the Louvre picture Freud associates to St Anne's smile the caressing figure of Leonardo's mother: to the similarity of age between St Anne and the Virgin he associates the rivalry between Leonardo's mother and his step-mother: and to the pyramidal form in which the two figures are enclosed he associates an attempt on Leonardo's part to reconcile "the two mothers of his childhood."

I have said enough, I hope, to show how misleading it is to say, as is sometimes said, that in the Leonardo essay Freud lays down a pattern for the explanation of art based on the model of dream-interpretation. It is true that with certain very definite qualifications Freud does in the course of this essay treat a number of works of art in just the way he would if they were dreams: the qualifications being that the associations he invokes are not free, and that the trains terminate on an already established complex. But there is nothing to suggest that Freud thought that this is the proper way to treat works of art if one wants to explain them as works of art: all we can safely conclude is that he thought this is a proper way to treat them if one wanted to use them as biographical evidence. There are, indeed, ancillary pieces of evidence to suggest that Freud's interest in the Leonardo essay was primarily biographical. This certainly is in accord with the reception that the original draft of the essay received—and presumably invited—when it was read to the Vienna Psychoanalytic Society a few months before its publication. The minutes reveal that in the discussion it was only Victor Tausk who referred to the paper as "a great critique of art" as well as a piece of psychoanalysis, and his remark went unheeded. Again, both in the original draft and in the final essay the feature most emphasized by Freud in Leonardo's works is certainly not an aesthetic feature: that they are very largely left unfinished. And, finally, it must be significant that Freud made virtually no attempt to identify in the work of the last phase any correlate to the fact that, though this phase too marks a regression, nevertheless it was a regression that enabled a new release of creativity.

If we now turn back from the Leonardo essay to the essay on the *Moses* of Michelangelo, with which I began, we find ourselves involved with a totally different enterprise. Indeed, if we consider both essays to be (roughly) studies in *expression*, then it looks as though they mark out the two ends of the spectrum of meaning that this term has occupied in European aesthetics. For, if the Leonardo essay concerns itself with expression in the modern sense— that is, with what the artist expresses in his works, or with Leonardo's expressiveness—then the Michelangelo essay is concerned with expression in the classical sense—that is, with what is expressed by the subject of the work, or the expressiveness of Moses. (The distinction is, of course, over-simple: and it is significant that there has been a continuous theory of expression in European aesthetics.)

Let us look for a moment at the problem that Michelangelo's great statue sets the physiognomically minded spectator. We may express it in a distinction used by Freud—and, of course, our aim anyhow is to get as close as possible to the problem as he conceived it—and ask initially whether *Moses* is a study of character or a study of action. Those critics who have favoured the latter interpretation have stressed the wrath of Moses and contended that the seated figure is about to spring into action and let loose his rage on the faithless Israelites. The wrath is evident, Freud argues, but the projected movement is not indicated in the statue and would moreover contradict the compositional plan of the tomb for which it was intended. Those critics who have favoured the former interpretation of the statue—that is, as a study in character—have stressed the passion, the strength, the force implicit in Michelangelo's representation. Such an interpretation can remain free of implausibility, but it seemed to Freud to leave too much of the detail of the statue uncovered and it insufficiently relates the inner to the outer. Freud's interpretation is that we should see the figure of Moses, not as being about to break out in rage, but as having checked a movement of anger. By seeing it as a study in suppressed action, that is self-mastery, we can also see it as a study in character and at the same time avoid any inconsistency with the compositional indications.

"Here we are fully back," Ernst Gombrich has written of this essay, "in the tradition of nineteenth-century art-appreciation:" and this tradition he partially characterized by referring to its preoccupation with the "spiritual content" of the work of art. The evident conservatism of Freud's method in the Michelangelo essay does in large measure warrant Gombrich's judgement, and yet I think that if we look carefully at Freud's text there are some scattered counter-indications that should warn us against taking it—what should I say?—too definitively.

It is a matter of more than local interest that in the Michelangelo essay Freud expresses his deep admiration for the critical writings of an art historian whom he had first encountered under the name of Ivan Lermolieff. This pseudonym, he later discovered, masked the identity of the great Giovanni Morelli, the founder of scientific connoisseurship. Now it was Morelli more than anyone else who brought the notion of "spiritual content" in art into disrepute. Admittedly what Morelli primarily objected to was not spiritual content as a criterion of value or of interpretation but its employment in determining the authorship of a particular painting: and it was to set this right that he devised his own alternative method, which consisted first in drawing up for each painter a schedule of forms, showing how he depicted the thumb, the lobe of the ear, the foot, the finger nail and other such trifles, and then in matching any putative work by a given painter against his particular schedule item by item. Nevertheless, once Morelli's method had been applied to determine authorship, the old idea of spiritual content had received a mauling from which it could not hope to recover.

It is, then, worth observing that it was precisely for his method, with all that it involved in the reversal of traditional aesthetic values, that Freud admired Morelli so much. Nor was Freud's admiration mere generality. Quite apart from the intriguing but quite unanswerable question whether the anonymity of the Michelangelo essay might not have had as one of its determinants an unconscious rivalry with Morelli, Freud would seem to have used in pursuit of physiognomy a method markedly like that which Morelli evolved to settle issues of connoisseurship. The somewhat self-conscious attention to minutiae, to measurement, to anatomical detail suggests that, even if Freud's critical aims were conservative, the methods he was prepared to envisage for achieving them were not so constricted. This point is one to which we may have to return. And, finally, it must be observed that Freud, both at the beginning and at the end of his essay, endeavours to link, though without indicating precisely how, the physiognomy of Moses with an intention of Michelangelo.

And now I want to turn to the third and only other extended essay that Freud wrote on art or an artist. (I exclude the Dostoevsky essay because, though almost the length of the *Moses* essay, it contains so little on its nominal subject.) In the summer of 1906 Freud had his attention drawn by Jung, whom he had not yet met, to a story by the north German playwright and novelist Wilhelm Jensen (1837-1911) entitled *Gradiva*. Though Freud later referred to the work as "having no particular merit in itself," which seems a fair judgement, it evidently intrigued him at the time and by May of the following year it had become the subject of an essay, "Delusions and Dreams in Jensen's *Gradiva*." Unfortunately in the Standard Edition of Freud's works the practice of the original English translation, of printing Jensen's story as well as Freud's text, has not been followed. The reader who relies upon Freud's résumé is unlikely to appreciate fully the deftness and subtlety with which he interprets the text: in the résumé text and interpretation are in such close proximity that we may take the interpretation for granted.

Jensen's *Gradiva* is subtitled "A Pompeian Fancy," and it tells the story of a young German archaeologist, Norbert Hanold, who has so withdrawn himself from the world that his only attachment is to a small Roman plaque of a girl walking with an elegant and distinctive step, which he had first seen in the museum of antiquities at Rome and of which he has bought a cast. He calls the girl Gradiva, he spins around her the phantasy that she came from Pompeii, and, after several weeks of quite vain research into her gait and its distinctiveness or otherwise, he sets off to Italy, heavily under the influence of a dream in which he watched Gradiva perish in the Pompeian earthquake. On his journey south life is made intolerable for him by the endless German honeymoon couples and by the flies. He hates, we may discern, the untidiness both of love and of life. Inevitably he drifts to Pompeii and the next day at noon, entering the house to which he has in phantasy assigned Gradiva, he sees the double of the girl who is represented in his beloved plaque. Are we to believe that this is a hallucination or a ghost? In fact it is neither; it is, as Norbert Hanold has to realize, a live person, though she continues to humour him in the belief that they knew each other in another life and that she has long been dead. There is another meeting, there are two further dreams, and all the while there is the pressure on Hanold of having to accept how much of his phantasy is proving to be real. Ultimately there is a revelation, by which time Hanold is prepared for the truth. The girl is a childhood friend of his who has always been in love with him. He, on the contrary, had repressed his love for her and had only allowed it to manifest itself in his attachment to the plaque, which, it now turned out, in so many of its treasured aspects, some of which had been projected by him on to it while others must have been the causes of his initial attraction to it, precisely reflected her. Even the name that he bestowed on the plaque, "Gradiva," was a translation of her name, "Bertgang." By the end of the story his delusion has been cast off, his repressed sexuality breaks through, and the girl has restored to her "her childhood friend who had been dug out of the ruins"—an image obviously of inexhaustible appeal to Freud, who was to draw upon it over and over again each time he elaborated his favoured comparison between the methods of psychoanalysis and the methods of archaeology.

It is natural to think of "Delusion and Dreams" as lying on the same line of inquiry as the later Michelangelo essay but at a point projected well beyond it. Both essays are studies in the character or mood or mind of the subject in a work of art, but in the Jensen essay the inquiry is pursued with what seems a startling degree of literalness. "A group of men," is how it begins, "who regarded it as a settled fact that the essential riddles of dreaming have been solved by the efforts of the author of the present work found their curiosity aroused one day by the question of the class of dreams that have never been dreamed at all—dreams created by imaginative writers and ascribed to invented characters in the course of a story." And Freud then proceeds to grapple with this question in such detail, giving a lengthy analysis of Hanold's two dreams, that the reader might feel, on reaching the last sentence of the essay, that it could profitably have come somewhat earlier. "But we must stop here," Freud writes, "or we may really forget that Hanold and Gradiva are only creatures of the author's mind."

But such a reaction on the part of the reader—or the feeling that Freud here is guilty of misapplying his technique of dream-interpretation because he has falsely assimilated characters of fiction to characters of real life—would be inappropriate. For it overlooks one important, and indeed surprising, fact: that Hanold's dreams *can* be interpreted, that there is sufficient evidence for doing so. Of course this fact is purely contingent, in that we could have no general reason to anticipate it. Nevertheless, it is so. The overall point might be brought out by comparing the dream-interpretations in the Jensen essay with that part of the Leonardo essay where, as we have seen, Freud sets out to interpret some of the late works of the painter somewhat on the analogy of dreams. Now, the former, it might be argued, compares unfavourably with the latter. For anyone who accepts the leading ideas of Freudian theory will agree that there must in principle be a way of eliciting the latent content of the Leonardo works: the two open questions being whether the evidence permits this to be done in practice and, if so, whether Freud succeeded in doing it. However, there can be no corresponding assurance that it is possible to elicit the content of Hanold's dreams: for Hanold's dreams are not actual dreams. Now, this argument is perfectly acceptable if what it points out is that there need not have been evidence adequate for the decipherment of Hanold's dreams. But Freud's discovery is that in point of fact there is: and this discovery is not only the presupposition on which the various dream-interpretations in the Jensen essay are based but also the most interesting feature about that essay.

Once this point is accepted, then Freud's effort to decipher the delusions and dreams of Norbert Hanold, so far from being merely the product of confusion between fiction and reality, can be seen as a genuine contribution to criticism. For it indicates the steps by which, explicitly to a certain kind of reader, implicitly to others, Hanold's beliefs and wishes are revealed—and in this respect it clearly refers to an aesthetic feature of *Gradiva*. And now an analogous point can be made for Freud's physiognomic researches into the Michelangelo *Moses*. For in this study Freud is to be seen, not simply as revealing to us the deepest mental layers of a particular representation, but as indicating how these layers, particularly the deepest of them, are revealed in the corresponding statue. And now perhaps we can see one way in which Freud diverges, if only in emphasis, from nineteenth-century appreciation. For Freud is at least as interested in the way in which the spiritual content of a work of art is made manifest as in the spiritual content itself: and when we take into account the "trivial" ways in which he thought deep content was most likely to manifest itself, the divergence visibly grows.

Let us stay for a moment with those arts in which revelation of character—of the character, that is, of the subject of the work, not as yet that of the artist—is a significant aesthetic feature. Now this feature cannot be unconstrained, otherwise it would cease to be of aesthetic interest. There must be some element in the work that at any rate slows down, or controls, the pace of revelation. Does Freud say anything about this other controlling factor—and the interrelation of the two? In *Gradiva* the controlling factor is not hard to identify: it is the growth of Norbert Hanold's self-consciousness or, as Freud calls it, his "recovery," which is in part an internal process and is in part effected through the agency of Gradiva. Now, Freud had an affection for this particular artistic compromise: it has a natural poignancy, and it also exhibits an obvious affinity with psychoanalytic treatment. As to the interrelation of the two factors, or how far the omniscient author is entitled to outrun his confused or unself-conscious characters, Freud has, implicitly at any rate, some interesting observations to make when he writes about the ambiguous remarks that abound in *Gradiva*. For instance, when Hanold first meets the seeming *revenant* from Pompeii, he says in reply to her first utterance: "I knew your voice sounded like that." Freud's suggestion is that the use of ambiguity by an author to reveal the character of his subject ahead of the process of self-knowledge is justified in so far as the ambiguously couched revelation corresponds to a repressed piece of self-knowledge.

Freud, however, has no desire to impose the pattern of revelation controlled by the rate of self-knowledge upon all art for which it makes sense. In perhaps his most interesting piece on art, a few pages entitled "Psychopathic Characters on the Stage," written in 1905 or 1906 but only published posthumously, Freud writes of those literary compositions in which the alternate current is supplied by action or conflict.

A relevant question that Freud deals with in this brief essay is, How explicit is to be our understanding of what is revealed to us? Freud's view is that it need not be explicit. Indeed, even in the most deeply psychological dramas, generations of spectators have found it difficult to say what it was that they understood. "After all," Freud writes engagingly, "the conflict in *Hamlet* is so effectively concealed that it was left to me to unearth it." Indeed Freud's point goes beyond this. It is not simply that our understanding need not be explicit but that in many cases there are dangers in explicitness, for explicitness could give rise to resistance if the character suffers from a neurosis which his audience shares with him. So here we have another virtue of what I have called the alternate current—namely that it serves what Freud calls "the diversion of attention." And one effective way in which it can do this is by plunging the spectator or the reader into a whirlpool of action from which he derives excitement while yet being secure from danger. And another contributory factor to this same end is the pleasure in play that is provided by the medium of the art: the element of "free play" that had been so heavily stressed in Idealist aesthetics.

And perhaps at this point we should just look back again for a moment at the Michelangelo essay. For we can now see a reason why in certain circumstances it might be, not merely just as acceptable, but actually better, that the revelation of expression should be achieved through small touches, through the trifles to which both Morelli and Freud, though for different reasons, attached such weight. For these trifles can more readily slip past the barriers of attention.

And now once again it is necessary to switch our point of view. For the diversion of attention as we have just been considering it would seem to belong to what might be called the "public relations" of the work of art. That is, its aim seems to be to secure popularity for the work or, more negatively, to avoid disapproval or even to evade censorship. However, if we now look at this process from the artist's point of view, we may be able to see how it can be regarded as contributing to the aesthetic character of the work. But first we must broaden our analysis somewhat. In the *History of the Psycho-Analytic Movement* Freud wrote: "The first example of an application of the analytic mode of thought to the problems of aesthetics was contained in my book on jokes." We have now grown familiar with the idea that *Jokes and their Relation to the Unconscious* could be made use of in explicating some of the problems of art, but it is perhaps insufficiently appreciated that the credit for this initiative must go to Freud himself.

Freud distinguished three levels to the joke, each marking a successive stage in its development. All three levels rest upon a primitive substrate of play, which initially comes into operation with the infantile acquisition of skills—specifically, so that we may single it out for attention, the skill of speech. Play generates what Freud calls functional pleasure, the pleasure derived from using idly, and thus exhibiting mastery over, a human capacity. Rising on this substrate, the lowest level is the *jest*, a piece of play with words or concepts with one and only one concession to the critical judgement: it makes sense. A jest is a playful way of saying something, but the something need be of no intrinsic interest. Where what is said claims interest in its own right, we move on to the second level and we have the *joke*. For the joke is constructed round a thought, though the thought, Freud insists, makes no contribution whatsoever to the pleasure that is specific to the joke. The pleasure—at any rate on the level with which we are concerned—derives entirely from the element of play, and the thought is there to give respectability to the whole enterprise by falsely claiming credit for the pleasure. And now we move to the third level—the *tendentious joke*. With the tendentious joke the whole machinery that we have so far considered—namely, the jest with a thought to protect it—is now used itself to protect a repressed purpose, either sexual or aggressive, which seeks discharge. But if we are to come to grips with this complex phenomenon, we must discriminate roles. Both jests and untendentious jokes are social practices, but their social side raises no real problems, nor is it of great significance. But with the tendentious joke it is significant. Let us see how this comes about. The joker makes use of the joke in order to divert his attention from the impulse that seeks expression, and the joke is expected to achieve this for him by the discharge of energy it can secure. But, unfortunately, the one person for whom the joke cannot perform this service is the joker: it is something to do with the fact that the joker has made the joke that prevents him from indulging freely in the possibility of play that it offers. The joke is incomplete in itself or, more straightforwardly, the joker cannot laugh at his own joke. Accordingly, if the joke is to fulfil the purpose of the tendentious joker, he requires a hearer to laugh at the joke—though, of course, the hearer, for his part, could never have laughed at it if he had made it himself. However, with the hearer, too, there is a danger, though the other way round: for it is the very openness of the invitation to play that might meet with censure if it is too blatantly extended. Hence the presence of the thought which is required to divert his attention from the play so that he may laugh at the joke. And his laughter licenses the joker in his ulterior purpose. In so far as the joke falls flat or is denied acclaim, the joker will feel unable to afford the repressed impulse the release he had surreptitiously promised it.

How far this analysis of the tendentious joke may be applied to art is uncertain, and perhaps it would be out of place to demand a general answer. There would seem, however, to be two respects in which a parallel holds. In the first place, what Freud calls the "radical incompleteness" of the joke parallels in psychological terms what is often called the institutional character of art—as well perhaps as suggesting the psychological machinery on which that institution rests. Art is (amongst other things) what is recognized as art, and Freud's account of the tendentious joke may allow us to see an extra reason why this should be so, as well as to make a new assessment of its importance. Secondly, there is a parallel between the uncertainty in the hearer of the joke about the source of his pleasure, and the diversion of attention that is predicated of the spectator of the work of art. And this should help to make it clear why "diversion of attention" should be an aesthetic aspect of the work of art, and not just a cheap bid for popularity.

At this point it is worth observing that we are now in a somewhat better position to consider the first of the two questions that arose out of my opening quotation—when I said, you will recall, that it was unclear how far Freud's emphasis on understanding as a prerequisite of appreciation was a purely personal avowal, or whether it indicated a theoretical position. We have now gone far enough to see that part of understanding how it is that a work of art affects us is recognizing the confusion or the ambiguity upon which this effect in part depends. One of the dangers in psychoanalysis, but also one of those against which it perennially warns us, is that in trying to be clear about our state of mind we may make the state of mind out to be clearer than it is.

Indeed, it looks as though the "diversion of attention" required of the spectator of the work of art is far more thoroughgoing than the corresponding demand made on the hearer of the joke. For the spectator not merely uses the overt content of the work of art to divert his attention from the element of play, he may also have to use the element of play to divert his attention from the more disturbing or latent content of the work of art. In this respect he combines in himself the roles of the maker and the hearer of the tendentious joke. Freud, in dissociating himself from the traditional theory that "intellectual bewilderment" is a necessary ingredient in the aesthetic attitude, may have prepared the way for an account of art and our attitude towards it more thoroughly and more deeply challenging to a naïvely rationalist view.

And this leads us to a large question, to which so much of this lecture has pointed. We might put it by asking, Is there, according to Freud, anything in the work of art parallel to the purpose that finds, or seeks, expression in so many of the other mental phenomena that Freud studied, and which variously provided models for his examination of art: the tendentious joke, the dream, the neurotic symptom? To this Freud's answer is, No. The artist certainly expresses himself in his work—how could he not? But what he expresses has not the simplicity of a wish or impulse.

Freud was guided in this by two rather elementary considerations, none the less important for that. The first is that the work of art does not have the immediacy or the directness of a joke or an error or a dream. It does not avail itself of some drop in attention or consciousness to become the sudden vehicle of buried desires. For all his attachment to the central European tradition of romanticism, a work of art remained for Freud what historically it had always been: a piece of work. And, secondly, art, at any rate in its higher reaches, did not for Freud connect up with that other and far broader route by which wish and impulse assert themselves in our lives: neurosis. "We forget too easily," Freud is reported as saying, "that we have no right to place neurosis in the foreground, wherever a great accomplishment is involved." The Minutes of the Vienna Psycho-analytic Society reveal him over and over again protesting against the facile equation of the artist and the neurotic. But once we abandon this equation, we lose all justification for thinking of art as exhibiting a single or unitary motivation. For outside the comparative inflexibility of the neurosis, there is no single unchanging form that our characters or temperaments assume. There are constant vicissitudes of feeling and impulse, constant formings and reformings of phantasy, over which it is certain very general tendencies pattern themselves: but with a flexibility in which, Freud suggests, the artist is peculiarly adept.

And, finally, we must remember that for Freud art, if expressive, was not purely expressive. It was also constructive. But here we come to a shortcoming or a lacuna in Freud's account of art which reduplicates one in his more general account of the mind, which was only slowly filled in. To understand this we have to look cursorily at the development of Freud's notion of the unconscious and unconscious mechanisms. Initially the notion of the unconscious enters Freud's theory in connection with repression. Then the notion proliferates, and the unconscious becomes identical with a mode of mental functioning called the primary process. Finally, Freud recognized that certain unconscious operations had a role which was not exhausted either by the contribution they made to defence, or by the part they played in the ongoing processes of the mind. They also had a constructive role to play in the binding of energy or, what is theoretically a related process, the building up of the ego. It was the study of identification, in which Freud included projection, that first led him to revise his views in this direction. But no shadow of this new development was cast over Freud's views on art, for the simple reason that there are not extended studies of art from this period. The unconscious appears in Freud's account of art only as providing techniques of concealment or possibilities of play. In a number of celebrated passages Freud equated art with recovery or reparation or the path back to reality. But nowhere did he indicate the mechanism by which this came about. By the time he found himself theoretically in a position to do so, the necessary resources of leisure and energy were, we must believe, no longer available to him.

LIONEL TRILLING

The Authentic Unconscious

I have not put forward the matter of our culture's adverse opinion of narration in order to deal with it as in itself it deserves to be dealt with, but only to exemplify the kind of cultural phenomena which might properly come within our purview. But now that it is before us, it may appropriately be made to serve a further purpose, that of introducing a large and difficult subject—the ideal of authenticity as it relates to the modern theory of the mind, and in particular to that concept which is definitive of modern psychological theory, the unconscious. The concept of the unconscious was brought to its present complex development by psychoanalysis. As I need scarcely say, psychoanalysis is a science which is based upon narration, upon telling. Its principle of explanation consists in getting the story told—somehow, anyhow—in order to discover how it begins. It presumes that the tale that is told will yield counsel.

Psychoanalysis entered fully upon the cultural scene not many years before Eliot made his statement about the novel having come to its end. Some critics have speculated that psychoanalysis itself played a part in the devolution of the novel, that it offered a narrative explanation of conduct which, by comparison with that of prose fiction, seemed more complete and authoritative. But if psychoanalysis can be thought to have been in competition with the novel and to have won some sort of ascendancy over it, this was not of long duration. Earlier I remarked on the fact that at present there is a withdrawal of credence from Freudian theory. This development cannot be ascribed to any single cause, but the contemporary disenchantment with narration as a way of explaining things surely has some bearing upon it.

Still, if a withdrawal of credence from psychoanalysis is indeed to be observed as a tendency of our culture, it is one which has by no means completed itself. Among the elements of Freudian theory there is at least one that stands in no danger of being abandoned, for it is integral to our cultural disposition. This is the doctrine that in the human mind there are two systems, one manifest, the other latent or covert. It is not an idea with which we are always at ease—the personal evidences of an unconscious mental system are likely to be received by each of us with an ever fresh surprise and discomfiture which qualify their credibility. Yet despite occasional vicissitudes, the idea of an unconscious mental system is firmly established in our culture.

That a portion of the activity of the mind is not immediately available to consciousness is of course not in itself a new idea. It did not originate with psychoanalysis. Freud himself said that it was the poets who discovered the unconscious, and beyond the poets' instinctive recognition of it there has been a considerable body of formulated belief in its existence and some fairly specific predications about its nature. Scholars have described the numerous pre-Freudian theories of the unconscious and a recent work by Henri F. Ellenberger, *The Discovery of the Unconscious*, does so in an especially thorough way.

In speaking of the sources of Freud's thought, Professor Ellenberger adduces an intellectual tendency which, he says, requires emphasis because it has hitherto been overlooked. This is the disposition of mind, salient in Europe for some centuries, which Ellenberger calls the "unmasking trend" and describes as "the systematic search for deception and self-deception and the uncovering of underlying truth." He assigns its beginnings to the French moralists of the seventeenth century and notes its continuance in Schopenhauer, Marx, Ibsen, and Nietzsche. I have spoken of the important part that the idea of "unmasking" played in the ethos of the French Revolution. The "unmasking trend" continues with unabated energy in our own time, and if we try to say why the idea that there is a mental system which lies hidden under the manifest system has won so wide an acceptance among us, doubtless one reason is that it accords with the firmly entrenched belief that beneath the appearance of every human phenomenon there lies concealed a discrepant actuality and that intellectual, practical, and (not least) moral advantage is to be gained by forcibly bringing it to light.

It would be an incomplete but not an inaccurate description of the theory of psychoanalysis to say that it conceives of the conscious system of the mind as a mask for the energies and intentions of the unconscious system. Freud himself puts it that the ego, which is the seat of consciousness, is "a kind of facade for the id," which is unconscious. This suggests a complicity between the ego and the id, which does in fact exist. It does not, however, suggest the antagonism that also exists between the two entities. The energies and intentions of the id are instinctual and libidinal and its sole aim is the achievement of pleasure. The primary concern of the ego is with the survival of the human organism, and to this end the ego undertakes to control the heedless energies and intentions of the id, going so far as to thrust them out of sight, which is to say, out of consciousness. By thus repressing the impulses of the id, the ego makes possible the existence of society, which is necessary for human survival.

But the tale, as we know all too well, does not end here. The instinctual drives of the id, although controlled and in large part repressed, do not acquiesce in the programme of the ego. In the darkness of the unconscious to which they are relegated, these drives maintain a complex subversive relation with the conscious system and succeed to some extent in expressing themselves through it, not directly but by means of a devious symbolism. This symbolic expression of the repressed instinctual drives typically involves some degree of pain and malfunction and is called neurosis. The pathology is universal among mankind. As Freud puts it, "We are all ill"—neurosis is of the very nature of the mind. Its intensity varies from individual to individual; in some the pain or malfunction caused by the symbolizing process is so considerable as to require clinical treatment. But the psychic dynamics of such persons are not different from those of the generality of mankind. We are all neurotic.

The clinical procedure of psychoanalysis is well known. The therapeutic method is based on the belief that when once the conscious part of the mind learns to interpret the difficult symbolism of the repressed drives of the unconscious and by this means brings to light what it feared and thrust out of sight, the ego will be able to confront the drives of the id in all their literalness and thus be relieved of the pain that their symbolic expression causes. The patient, the analysand, by various means—by retrieving his childhood experience, by reporting his dreams and interpreting them with the analyst's help, by articulating his fantasies and his fugitive thoughts, of which some will be trivial and silly, others shameful—will learn to identify the subversive devices of the banished impulses and come to terms with them as appropriate elements of his nature, thus depriving them of their power over him.

The therapeutic process of psychoanalysis would seem to constitute a very considerable effort of self-knowledge, a strenuous attempt to identify and overcome in the mental life of the individual an inauthenticity which is not the less to be deplored because it is enforced and universal. And this is so not only by reason of the nature of what has been concealed and is now to be discovered, because, that is, the idea of authenticity readily attaches itself to instinct, especially libidinal instinct, but also because a profound inauthenticity of the mental life is implied by the nature of neurosis, by its being a disguised substitute for something else. Psychoanalysis speaks of the pain or malfunction of neurosis as a "substitutive gratification"—what could be more inauthentic than an impulse towards pleasure which gains admission into consciousness by masquerading as its opposite? The neurosis is a Tartuffian deceit practised by one part of the mind upon another. It is to be dealt with by a minute investigation of its machinations which will lead to tearing the mask from its face.

This enterprise does not in itself constitute the whole of the psycho-analytical therapy or suggest the full extent of the developed theory of the neurosis. Yet it expresses what might be called the initiating principle of Freud's system and as such it is singled out by Jean-Paul Sartre to bear the brunt of the adverse judgement he passes upon psychoanalysis, which holds that the psychoanalytical enterprise of tracking down and exposing the inauthenticity of the mental life is itself ineluctably inauthentic.

Sartre delivers this opinion in the well-known second chapter of *Being and Nothingness*, his monumental and compulsive research into the conditions of personal authenticity. The chapter is entitled "Bad Faith," a term which the translator of the work in her "Key to Special Terminology" defines in part as "a lie to oneself within the unity of a single consciousness." The psychoanalytical transaction with the clandestine instinctual drives is said by Sartre to be open to the imputation of this falsehood in two respects. One bears upon the moral consequences of the mental dualism which psychoanalysis assumes, the other upon what may be described as the intentional naïveté with which psychoanalysis interprets the prevarications of the psychic mechanism it postulates.

The dualism to which Sartre refers is that of the unconscious id, which is wholly comprised of the instinctual drives, and the conscious ego. "By the distinction between the 'id' and the 'ego,'" Sartre says, "Freud has cut the psychic whole into two." The bad faith of psychoanalysis follows from this dichotomy. It consists of one part of the psychic whole regarding the other part as an object and thereby disclaiming responsibility for it. This disclaimer is implicit in the circumstance that the activities of the id can be known to the ego only by hypothesis, as more or less probable; they cannot be known with the force of an intuition, of a felt experience, as an actual part of the individual's moral being. As Sartre puts it, "I *am* the ego but I *am not* the id," which is to say, "I am my own psychic phenomena in so far as I establish them in their conscious reality." The person in psychoanalytic treatment is inducted into a view of the psyche according to which he, the ego-he, the subject, is to take cognizance of part of his mental life not in its "conscious reality," not as an intuition, but as an object. The psychic facts which are made manifest to him, although they are represented as being of decisive importance in their effect upon him, he apprehends as external phenomena, having their existence apart from the consciousness which constitutes his being. "I am not these psychic facts," Sartre says, "in so far as I receive them passively . . . ," that is, in so far as he receives them as objects. And not only are the psychic facts of the id received passively by the ego, they are received with but limited credence—"I am not these psychic facts, in so far as I . . . am obliged to resort to hypotheses about their origin and true meaning, just as the scholar makes conjectures about the nature and essence of an external phenomenon." The criterion of the truth of these hypotheses is "the number of conscious psychic facts which it explains," but its explanation can never have the certainty of intuitions. Psychoanalysis, in sum, so far from advancing the cause of personal authenticity, actually subverts it in a radical way through the dichotomy it institutes in the mental life, one of whose elements is consigned to a mere objective existence, hypothetical into the bargain, for which the subject is not answerable.

Presumably it would not weigh with Sartre that psychoanalysis in its clinical practice seeks to overcome the dualism it is said to postulate, making it a desideratum that the psychic facts disclosed to the analysand shall have for him the force of an intuition, of a felt experience, and as such be made part of his subjectivity. Inevitably the extent of the subjectivization falls short of completeness and some part of the psychic facts remains in an unregenerate state of existence as an object.

The second line of argument which Sartre takes in bringing into question the authenticity of psychoanalysis bears upon the nature of the "censor," which stands between the consciousness of the ego and the subversive libidinal energies of the id and prevents the latter from making themselves directly manifest. This agent of repression is represented by psychoanalysis as belonging to the unconscious part of the mental life, and it is Sartre's point that this definition of it is false, because in order to carry out its function, the censor must engage in purposive acts of perception and discrimination which are of the very nature of consciousness. ". . . It is not enough that it discern the condemned drives; it must also apprehend them as *to be repressed*, which implies in it at the very least an awareness of its activity. In a word, how could the censor discern the impulses needing to be repressed without consciousness of them? How can we conceive of a knowledge which is ignorant of itself? To know is to know that one knows, said Alain. Let us rather say that all knowing is a consciousness of knowing." The conclusion is that the censor must have a consciousness of "being conscious of the drive to be repressed, but precisely in order not to be conscious of it." For psychoanalysis to base its explanations upon an agent of the mental life to which such double-dealing can be ascribed is surely bad faith at its worst.

It is to be observed that in *Being and Nothingness* Sartre deals with the theory of psychoanalysis in a relatively early stage in its development. Writing in 1943, he takes no account of the changes that had been going on in Freud's thought for almost a quarter-century. In 1919 Freud began a radical revision of his theory of the unconscious, especially of the ego. The new formulations make anachronistic Sartre's description of the way Freud cuts the psychic whole into two, for it can no longer be said that the dichotomy he institutes is that of the conscious ego and the unconscious id. On the basis of the older theory Sartre had been justified in understanding the ego to be synonymous with the conscious self, but in Freud's drastic modification of his former view the ego is no longer repesented as being coextensive with consciousness: some part of the ego is now said to be as far out of sight in the darkness of the unconscious as the id itself. "There is something in the ego," Freud says, "which is also unconscious, which behaves exactly like the repressed—that is, which produces poweful effects without being itself conscious and which requires special work before it is made conscious."

What is more, the ego is no longer viewed as "something autonomous and unitary" and in this character as wholly antagonistic to the id. Rather, Freud says, the ego in its unconscious part is "continued without sharp limitation" into the id. "The ego itself is cathected with libido," and so intimate is the involvement of the two psychic entities, once thought to be nothing but hostile to each other, that Freud can say of the ego that it "is the libido's home and remains to some extent its headquarters."

There is yet another modification of the earlier account of the ego. To Freud's surprise—he speaks of the phenomenon as a "strange" one—the activities which go on in the unconscious part of the ego are the same as some of the activities which the conscious part of the ego characteristically engages in. These are activities which are regarded as, to use Freud's phrase, "extremely high ones," such as moral judgement and self-criticism.

The momentousness of Freud's revision of his theory of the ego will be immediately apparent. Where once the ego, the segment of the mind which, so to speak, does the living and transacts business with the world, was thought of as wholly conscious and bedevilled in its practical purposive existence by the blind instinctual drives which seek to subvert it, now the ego is understood to be in part unavailable to consciousness, no less devious than the id and profoundly implicated with the id's libidinal energies, while at the same time its "extremely high" activities of moral judgement and self-criticism direct themselves not only upon the id but also upon the conscious part of itself.

There would seem to be no element of the new theory, supposing Sartre to have been aware of it, which is calculated to qualify his position on the inherent inauthenticity of psychoanalysis. To be sure, we have seen that it can no longer be charged against Freud that he cuts the psychic whole into two in the particular way that Sartre complains of. But if the dualism of subject-ego and object-id has been done away with, we now have the larger and more portentous dualism of conscious ego as subject and unconscious ego as object, with all the import of inauthenticity it has for the phenomenological and existential position, of which Sartre's chapter may stand as the paradigm. As for Freud's having identified the agent of censorship as the unconscious part of the ego, to which he attributes the activities of moral judgement and self-criticism, it would seem to confirm Sartre's contention that the unconscious is not properly to be so designated, for by definition these "extremely high" activities are based upon knowing, which, equally by definition, is consciousness of knowing.

The imputed contradiction cannot be thought a source of distress to the psychoanalytic theory. It may be said, indeed, that the tendency of the later development of Freud's thought is exactly to assign to the unconscious, specifically to the ego, those traits of perception, of knowing, which are implied by intention. If this leads to the necessity of characterizing as conscious what psychoanalysis terms "the unconscious," the contradiction is one of terminology rather than of conception. The good faith of psychoanalysis is not impugned if the situation it postulates is described as being that of two consciousnesses, one of which is not accessible to the other by intuition.

The increased degree of systematic intentionality which psychoanalysis had discovered in what it designates as the unconscious did not make any the easier the task of bringing it into the comprehension of what it calls the conscious. On the contrary: the extreme complication of the topography and dynamics of the ego and the "special work" it called for gave pause to the earlier therapeutic optimism of psychoanalysis, at least in point of the length of time required for successful treatment, leading Freud to write his paper with the disquieting title, "Analysis Terminable and Interminable." The increased refractoriness of the unconscious is to be laid at the door of a newly discerned principle of inauthenticity, the extent of whose duplicity is suggested by its success in appropriating the reason and authority of society for its own self-serving purposes. The virtually resistless power of this principle of inauthenticity is the informing idea of Freud's mature social theory.

From the first, it need scarcely be said, a conception of society had been central to Freud's psychology. The ego was a social entity; society was the field of its experience and from society the ego took much of its direction and received many of its gratifications. In relation to the id, which was defined by its a-social impulses, the ego was the surrogate of society. One might say that society was all too rigorous in its demands and that at its hands the ego as well as the id of any of its individual members suffered excessive frustration. Still, the social life had come into being at the behest of the ego and to serve its purpose of survival. The price which society exacted for advancing the aims of the ego could be scrutinized and possibly adjusted. Psychoanalysis certainly did not license the idea that communal life and the civilization that arose from it could be changed in any essential way, to the end of freeing the individual from frustration, yet it did seem to suggest that the relation between the individual and the community was, roughly speaking, a contractual one, which the individual might regard pragmatically. It was a relation that seemed to admit of at least some degree of accommodation on both sides.

But this view of the cause of individual frustration was profoundly modified by the development of Freud's new conception of the ego. In 1930 Freud published his most fully articulated statement of what his theory of the mind implies for man's social destiny. *Civilization and Its Discontents* is a work of extraordinary power. For social thought in our time its significance is unique. It may be thought to stand like a lion in the path of all hopes of achieving happiness through the radical revision of social life.

Despite Freud's gift of lucid expression, *Civilization and Its Discontents* is a difficult book, in some part because it undertakes to lead us beyond an idea with which we are familiar and comfortable, that society is the direct and "sufficient" cause of man's frustration. Its central thesis is that society is no more than the "necessary" cause of frustration. As Freud now describes the dynamics of the unconscious, the direct agent of man's unhappiness is an element of the unconscious itself. The requirements of civilization do indeed set in train an exigent disciplinary process whose locus is the ego, but this process, Freud says in effect, is escalated by the unconscious ego far beyond the rational demands of the societal situation. The informing doctrine of *Civilization and Its Discontents* is that the human mind, in the course of instituting civilization, has so contrived its own nature that it directs against itself an unremitting and largely gratuitous harshness.

The specific agent of this extravagant severity is an element of the unconscious which has not been named in what I have so far said about psychoanalysis, although its activities have been referred to—they are those "extremely high ones" of moral judgement and self-criticism. The element of the unconscious that carries on these activities Freud calls the superego. He tells us that the superego was originally part of the ego but seceded from it to establish an autonomous existence and a position of dominance over the ego's activities. It derives its authority from society, whose psychic surrogate it in some sense is. In some sense only, however, because in point of repressiveness the superego is far more severe than society, whose purposes are largely practical and therefore controlled by reason. We mistake the nature of the superego when we make it exactly synonymous, as we commonly do, with conscience. Only up to a point are the two coextensive. The operations of conscience are determined by its practical social intentions, but the superego is under no such limitation and in consequence its activity is anything but rational. The process it has instituted against the ego is largely gratuitous, beyond the needs of reason and beyond the reach of reason. The particular kind of pain it inflicts is that which Freud calls guilt.

We must be clear that in Freud's use of it this notorious word does not have its ordinary meaning. Freud does not use it to denote the consciousness of wrong-doing, which he calls remorse. The nature of guilt as Freud conceives it is precisely that it does not originate in actual wrong-doing and that it is not conscious. It takes its rise from an unfulfilled and repressed wish to do wrong, specifically the wrong of directing aggression against a sacrosanct person, originally the father, and it is experienced not as a discrete and explicit emotion but as the negation of emotion, as anxiety and depression, as the diminution of the individual's powers and the perversion of the intentions of his conscious ego, as the denial of the possibility of gratification and delight, even of desire. Guilt is Blake's worm at the root of the rosetree.

At this point I think it should be remarked that the description of the superego given in *Civilization and Its Discontents* is—by conscious intention, of course—a highly prejudicial one, putting all possible emphasis upon the gratuitousness of its behaviour, upon its lack of measure and reason, its needless harshness. As against this pejorative view, we should recall that Freud understood the institution of the superego to be a decisive "advance" in the development of the mind. "It is in keeping with the course of human development that external coercion gradually becomes internalized," he says in *The Future of an Illusion*; "for a special mental agency, man's superego, takes it over. . . . Every child presents this process of transformation to us; only by that means does it become a moral and social being. Such a strengthening of the superego is a most precious cultural asset in the psychological field. Those in whom it has taken place are turned from being opponents of civilization into being its vehicles. The greater their number is in a cultural unit the more secure is its culture and the more it can dispense with external measures of coercion."

Yet when we have given all possible recognition to the essential and beneficent part that the superego plays in the creation and maintenance of civilized society, we cannot ignore its deplorable irrationality and cruelty. These traits manifest themselves in an ultimate form in the terrible paradox that although the superego demands renunciation on the part of the ego, every renunciation which the ego makes at its behest, so far from appeasing it, actually increases its severity. The aggression which the ego surrenders is appropriated by the superego to intensify its own aggression against the ego, an aggression which has no motive save that of its own aggrandizement. The more the ego submits to the superego, the more the superego demands of it in the way of submission.

It is not practicable to recapitulate here Freud's explanation of how the superego became what it now is—the argument is difficult in the extreme, involving as it does the contradictions and conversions of the immemorial dialectic between the fostering and unifying instinct which Freud calls Eros and the hypothesized death-instinct from which aggression derives. And for our purpose, the whole of the dark history, fascinating though it be, is not essential. It will be enough if we understand that although it was to serve the needs of civilization that the superego was installed in its disciplinary office, its actual behaviour was not dictated by those needs; the movement of the superego from rational pragmatic authority to gratuitous cruel tyranny was wholly autonomous.

This being so, must we not say that Freud's theory of the mind and of society has at its core a flagrant inauthenticity which it deplores but accepts as essential in the mental structure? Man's existence in civilization is represented as being decisively conditioned by a psychic entity which, under the mask of a concern with social peace and union, carries on a ceaseless aggression to no purpose save that of the enhancement of its own power, inflicts punishment for no act committed but only for a thought denied, and, so far from being appeased by acquiescence in its demands, actually increases its severity in the degree that it is obeyed. Nor does the insatiable tyrant confine its operations to the internal life of individuals; its rage for peaceableness quickens and rationalizes man's rage against man. The hegemony of this ferocious idol of the psychic cave may indeed not have been required or intended by civilization, but surely in tolerating the great fraud civilization is profoundly implicated in its grotesque inauthenticity.

It is natural to suppose that if this anomalous condition of human existence can be discovered and described by the rational intellect, it might, by this same agency, be dealt with to the end of controlling its activity and thus bringing about a substantial increase of human happiness. Inevitably we entertain the speculation that, since the aggressivity of the superego has some part of its tortuous etiology in its response to the aggressive impulses of the ego, a revision of societal arrangements which would have the effect of lessening ego-aggression might induce the superego to abate its characteristic fierceness. Freud himself, in the concluding pages of *Civilization and Its Discontents*, raises the question of how far this project is susceptible of being realized. The reply he makes is tentative and gentle in its manner, as how could it not be, denying as it does an aspiration to which all of conscious human desire must tend? He will not dismiss out of hand the possibility of devising societal forms which might have a beneficent effect upon the psychic dynamics he has described. But his scepticism, though muted in courtesy to our hope, is profound—is, we cannot but know, entire. He consents to say that it is "quite certain that a real change in the relation of human beings to possessions" would make society's ethical ideals more easily attainable. He cannot go on to say that this will bring about a melioration of the dynamics of the unconscious life. He understands the limitless exigence of the superego to be rooted in the timeless past, in the natural history of an organism in which the ceaseless effort to survive is matched in strength by the will to find peace in extinction. Against the psychic dynamics produced by this ambivalence, this interfusion of the primal Yes and the no less primal No, and reinforced by later ambivalences such as the simultaneous love and hate of the father and the desire for both isolate autonomy and for union with others, it is unlikely that any revision of societal forms can prevail. Ultimately it is a given of biology, definitive of man's nature, and its consequences are not to be reversed.

Why did Freud bring his intellectual life to its climax—for such we must take *Civilization and Its Discontents* to be—with this dark doctrine? What was his motive in pressing upon us the ineluctability of the pain and frustration of human existence?

The question I put is the one that Nietzsche says should guide our dealings with any systematic thinker. He urges us to look below the structure of rational formulation to discover the *will* that is hidden beneath, and expressed through, its elaborations. What is that will up to? What does it want—really want, that is, apart from the "truth" that it says it wants?

There is no malice in the question Nietzsche prescribes. It has for its purpose not "reduction" but comprehension, such grasp upon a man's thought as may come through the perception of its unarticulated and even unconscious intention. It is a mode of critical investigation whose propriety and efficiency Freud himself of course confirms.

To that question I would propose this answer: that Freud, in insisting upon the essential immitigability of the human condition as determined by the nature of the mind, had the intention of sustaining the authenticity of human existence that formerly had been ratified by God. It was his purpose to keep all things from becoming "weightless."

For Freud, as we know, religion was an illusion with no future whatever. This certitude was central to his world-view and he was remorseless in his efforts to enforce it. Yet from religion as it vanished Freud was intent upon rescuing one element, the imperative actuality which religion attributed to life. Different individual temperaments, committed to incompatible cultural predilections, will respond to *Civilization and Its Discontents* in diverse ways, but all will take into account, positively or negatively, its powerful representation of the momentous claim which life makes upon us, by very reason, it seems, of its hardness, intractability, and irrationality. The fabric of contradictions that Freud conceives human existence to be is recalcitrant to preference, to will, to reason; it is not to be lightly manipulated. His imagination of the human condition preserves something—much—of the stratum of hardness that runs through the Jewish and Christian traditions as they respond to the hardness of human destiny. Like the Book of Job it propounds and accepts the mystery and the naturalness—the natural mystery, the mysterious naturalness—of suffering. At the same time it has at its heart an explanation of suffering through a doctrine of something like original sin: not for nothing had Freud in his youth chosen John Milton as a favourite poet, and although of course the idea of redemption can mean nothing to him, he yet acquiesces, and with something of Milton's appalled elation, in the ordeal of man's life in history.

Nothing could be further from my intention than to suggest that Freud's attitude to human experience is religious. I have it in mind only to point to the analogy which may be drawn between Freud's response to life and an attitude which, although it is neither exclusive to nor definitive of religion, is yet, as it were, contained in religion and sustained by it. This is what we might call the tragic element of Judaism and Christianity, having reference to the actual literary genre of tragedy and its inexplicable power to activate, by the representation of suffering, a faith quite unrelated to hope, a piety that takes virtually the form of pride—however harsh and seemingly gratuitous a fate may be, the authenticity of its implicit significance is not to be denied, confirmed as it is by the recognition of *some* imperative which has both brought it into being and prescribed its acceptance, and in doing so affirmed the authenticity of him to whom the fate is assigned. It is this authenticating imperative, irrational and beyond the reach of reason, that Freud wishes to preserve. He locates it in the dialectic of Eros and death, which is the beginning of man's nature. Its force in his own life, in the shaping of its character and style, was decisive. In the last days of his long painful illness Freud forbade his physician to administer any anodyne stronger than aspirin, and when he discovered that his injunction had been violated out of compassion, he flashed out in anger, *"Bei welchem Recht?"*: *by what right* had the good Dr. Schur interfered with his patient's precious sentiment of being as that was defined by his chosen relation to his fate, with—as a phrase in *Beyond the Pleasure Principle* has it—the organism's "wish to die in its own way"? That bitter rebuke had its origin in assumptions that are now archaic. The perception of their inevitable anachronism, of their ever-diminishing vitality, was the ground of Nietzsche's revulsion from the developing modern culture. Nietzsche dreaded the "weightlessness of all things," the inauthenticity of experience, which he foresaw would be the consequence of the death of God. Hence his celebration of what he called the "energizing pessimism" of the Greeks in their great day, hence his passionate recommendation of *amor fati*, which might be translated by a phrase of Marx's, "the appropriation of human reality" which includes, Marx said, human suffering, "for suffering humanly considered is an enjoyment of the self for man."

JEAN LAPLANCHE

The Order of Life and the Genesis of Human Sexuality

Our point of reference in discussing sexuality in psychoanalysis will be Freud's fundamental and resolutely innovative text *Three Essays on the Theory of Sexuality*. The importance the author attributed to that work is manifest in the frequency with which he modified it: in reeditions of 1910, 1915, 1920, and 1924-25, revised on each occasion in the very detail of its sentences and terminology, with additions which simultaneously preserve the original organization of the work and open it up to later discoveries. There are, in addition, copious notes, particularly for the final, 1924 version, which is contemporaneous with the "last theory of drives." It is in these strata and repetitions that the evolution and enrichment of the theory of sexuality may be best situated. But since we have just alluded to a last turning point, the final version—in the sense in which a "version" constitutes as well a way of reversing a work, a turning point—that final version, begun in 1920, is inscribed only minimally in the text itself, with the exception of the footnotes. So that if one wanted an approximate idea of what the *Three Essays* might have been had they been first undertaken in 1920, one would do best to consult a text like the *Outline of Psychoanalysis* (1938), and specifically its third chapter. And yet even in so late a text as the *Outline*, one senses the immense difficulty experienced by Freud in proposing a synthesis, as though his final contribution—concerning Eros and the death drive—could but barely be integrated into the first notion of sexuality.

For the *Three Essays* do not present an abstract theory of drives in general, but describe instead that drive par excellence: the sexual drive. So

Translated by Jeffrey Mehlman. From *Life and Death in Psychoanalysis*. Copyright © 1976 by the Johns Hopkins University Press.

much so, in fact, that without pretending to remain faithful (through some falsely eclectic synthesis) to the *entirety* of what Freud may have said concerning drives, we may claim, nevertheless, to follow the dominant line of his thought in offering a thesis which will recur throughout our argument: *it is sexuality which represents the model of every drive and probably constitutes the only drive in the strict sense of the term.* And if it is indeed true that, after 1920, Freud proposes and supports a theory englobing *two types* of drives, and links sexuality with one of them—with that biological, even cosmological force he then calls Eros—it is at that point that our thesis will seem most openly in contradiction with Freud's thought, but it is precisely at that juncture as well that a series of difficulties will also surface in Freud's own work.

In our first development, we will confine ourselves to sexuality as it constitutes the object of the *Three Essays*. In any effort to grasp what is, in fact, at stake in that text, nothing is more instructive than a glance at its organization: an apparently simple scheme, in three parts: sexual aberrations, infantile sexuality, the transformations of puberty. And yet were one to reconstitute a detailed table of contents, the greatest complication would result. That complexity is, of course, in part due to interpolations dating from different kinds of arrangement: a level one might term heuristic (following the genesis of psychoanalytic discovery itself), a polemical level (destroying the accepted conception of sexuality), a genetic level (retracing its emergence within the human being). We shall attempt to delineate how these three different levels may be articulated, how specifically the movement of Freud's thought, the heuristic level, follows—as in every profound exercise of thought—the movement of the "thing itself": a truth it was Hegel's to have rendered explicit.

The guiding thread in our study will be the notion of *drive (Trieb)*, and the pair it forms with a second term: *instinct*. If it is true in general that terminology, and above all its transposition from one language to another, can guide—but also misguide—us, problems of translation have introduced in the present case a confusion which is far from having disappeared. Whence our concern that the following remarks not be attributed simply to the meticulousness of a translator. *Trieb* has frequently been translated in French as *instinct*, and transposed by psychoanalysts in English, as well, as *instinct*. Yet we encounter in Freud, and in the German language in general, not one but two terms, two "signifiers," to use a more recent terminology. Two signifiers then, and it may be said that in common usage they have more or less the same meaning, just as their etymologies are parallel: *Trieb* comes from *treiben*, "to push"; *Instinkt* finds its origin in Latin, from *instinguere*, which also means "to incite," "to push." But—as frequently the case with languages and especially with German—when faced with a doublet of this type, an author approaching latent inflections of vocabulary with all the seriousness they deserve will attempt to exploit such objective duplicity in order to introduce a slight difference of meaning, which is occasionally barely perceptible, but will at times be accentuated to the point of constituting a veritable opposition. Such is the case with *Trieb* ("drive") and *Instinkt* ("instinct"): two terms which are employed by Freud even if, unfortunately, it has been insufficiently noted that the term *Instinkt* is used to designate something entirely different from what is described elsewhere as sexuality. *Instinkt*, in Freud's language, is a preformed behavioral pattern, whose arrangement is determined hereditarily and which is repeated according to modalities relatively adapted to a certain type of object. More important than etymology then, more important even than their semantic resonances in German culture, we discover a certain relation between meanings assumed by the two terms in Freud's scientific discovery, a complex relation, comprising an *analogy*, a *difference*, and also a *derivation* from one to the other. This is a derivation which is not simply conceptual, but which we may, with Freud, relate to a real derivation: the derivation in man of drives from instincts.

First their analogy: it is based on a common substrate in the analysis of the concept. The analysis of a drive, as it is presented to us in its elements, is also valid, in its generality, for an instinct. That analysis is sketched out, through successive approximations, in the course of different editions of the *Three Essays*, but in order to find a more systematic presentation, one had best consult a later text, "Instincts and Their Vicissitudes." There, the drive is decomposed according to four dimensions or, as Freud puts it, according to the four "terms which are used in reference to the concept of a drive": "impetus" *(Drang)*, "aim" *(Ziel)*, "object" *(Objekt)*, and "source" *(Quelle)*.

The *impetus*, he first tells us, is the motor factor in the drive, "the amount of force or the measure of the demand for work which it represents. The character of exercising pressure is common to all drives; it is in fact their very essence." These lines are exemplary in their reference to mechanics and, more precisely, to dynamics, which will always remain central for Freud. What is called the economic point of view in psychoanalysis is quite precisely that of a "demand for work": if there is work, a modification in the organism, it is because ultimately there is an exigency, a force; and, as in the physical sciences, force can be defined only through the measure of a quantity of work. To define a drive by its impetus, a *Trieb* by its *Drang*, is, from an epistemological point of view, almost a tautology: the latter is but the hypostasized, abstract element of the former. So that, to anticipate what will follow, we would propose the following hypothesis: it is that abstract element alone, the economic factor, which will remain constant in the derivation that will bring us from instincts to drives.

The *aim* now. It is, Freud tells us in the *Three Essays*, "the act to which the drive is driven." Thus, in the case of a preformed instinct, it is the motory scheme, the series of acts which results in a certain accomplishment. What precisely is that accomplishment? If we refer this time to the text "Instincts and Their Vicissitudes," we see that this accomplishment is always the same and ultimately rather monotonous; the only "final" aim is always satisfaction, defined in the most general way: the appeasing of a certain tension caused precisely by the *Drang*, that pressure we have been speaking about. The question then arises of determining the relation between an aim which is entirely general and (as with "impetus") abstract—the appeasing of tension—and, on the other hand, the very specific and determined acts which are the aims of various instincts: eating, seeing (since one finds in Freud a "drive to see"), making love, etc. The problem is that of the specification of the aim: why is it that something quite specific and not simply appeasement represents the *final aim?*

If we pursue the analysis, drawing on different texts of Freud, we discover that the aim of the drive constantly calls into play the following two factors: at times the object, at others, the source. The *object*: to the extent that Freud and, after him, virtually all psychoanalysts gradually came to focus on the notion of "object relations," which represents a kind of synthetic point of view between, on the one hand, a type of activity, the specific mode of a particular drive action, and on the other hand, its privileged object. Thus orality, to take the first example of a drive, implies both a certain mode of relation, say incorporation, and a certain type of object, one which is capable of being swallowed or incorporated. We encounter here a first possible elaboration of the notion of aim, its specification by its *source*; and here, apparently (we will soon see that the theory is in fact more complex) a far more biologistic and vitalistic orientation seems to prevail.

We shall examine, then, in greater detail these two concepts: *object* and *source*. Object of the drive? In order to eliminate rapidly certain misconceptions, we shall recall first that such an object is not necessarily an inanimate one, a thing: the Freudian *Objekt* is not opposed in essence to subjective being. No "objectification" of the love relation is intended. If in the classical language of the French seventeenth century, the term was already used to designate the focus of passion—*flamme, ressentiment*—it is in that rather broad sense that our "object" should be understood. And yet our caution against a vulgarized concept of the love object ("You treat me like an object," as the phrase goes) should not be taken as absolute. One perceives this simply by following the movement of its "definition" in the *Three Essays*. Temporarily, in the introduction, the "sexual object" is defined as "the person from whom sexual attraction proceeds." But the analysis of sexual aberrations results in an inversion of this point of view:

> It has been brought to our notice that we have been in the habit of regarding the connection between the sexual drive and the sexual object as more intimate than it in fact is. Experience of the cases that are considered

abnormal has shown us that in them the sexual instinct and the sexual object are merely soldered together—a fact which we have been in danger of overlooking in consequence of the uniformity of the normal picture, where the object appears to form part and parcel of the drive. We are thus warned to loosen the bond that exists in our thoughts between drive and object. It seems probable that the sexual drive is in the first instance independent of its object; nor is its origin likely to be due to its object's attractions.

Thus, despite our reservations, the term *object* appears initially to designate something which functions as a means: "the thing in regard to which or through which the drive is able to achieve its aim." There is a priority of satisfaction and of the satisfying action in relation to that "in regard to which" that action finds its conclusion. This brings us to a familiar problem in psychoanalytic thought, which might be termed summarily the "contingency" of the object. Insofar as the object is that "in which" the aim finds its realization, the specificity or individuality of the object is, after all, of minimal concern; it is enough for it to possess certain *traits* which trigger the satisfying action; in itself, it remains relatively indifferent and contingent.

An additional dimension of the object in psychoanalysis is that it is not necessarily an object in the sense of the theory of knowledge: an "objective" object. We might here distinguish clearly two meanings which unfortunately, in recent psychoanaytic theory, are too often in a state of coalescence: the notion of objectivity in the sense of knowledge and the notion of objectality in which the object, this time, is an object of the drive and not a scientific or perceptual object. I point this out in order to emphasize that the object of the drive can be, without prejudice, a *fantasmatic* object and that it is perhaps essentially such.

Finally, to conclude this series of clarifications, we should insist that the object is not necessarily a "total" person; it may be a *partial* (or *component*) object, in the phrase introduced by Melanie Klein but found—and quite early—at the center of Freud's thought. Partial objects include breast, penis, and numerous other elements related to bodily life (excrement, child, etc.), all of which have in common the fundamental characteristic of being, in fact or in fantasy, *detached or detachable*.

In concluding this analysis of the notion of *drive*, we will focus our attention at great length on the term *source*. If, in the *Three Essays*, the definition of a source—as we shall soon see—is relatively complex and ambiguous, in the text "Instincts and Their Vicissitudes," to which reference has been made collaterally, it is univocal: the *Quelle* is an unknown but theoretically knowable somatic process, a kind of biological x, whose psychical translation would in fact be the drive. by the "source of a drive" is meant "that somatic process in an organ or part of the body from which there results a stimulus represented in mental life by a drive." We note here the term *represented*, a fundamental articulation of Freud's metapsychology, which the limits of this presentation do not allow us to elaborate: suffice it to observe that the most frequent model used by Freud to account for the relation between the somatic and the psychical employs the metaphor of a kind of "delegation" provided with a mandate that need not be absolutely imperative. Thus a local biological stimulus finds its delegation, its "representation" in psychical life as a drive. We do not know whether the somatic process in question is of a strictly chemical nature, or whether it corresponds as well to a release of other (e.g., mechanical) forces: the study of the sources of drives, Freud concludes, "lies outside the scope of psychology," and the problem might eventually be solved by biology. Thus we encounter the central problem of our own study: the relation to the science of life.

We shall return in a moment to the question of the source, which seems particularly interesting as the point of articulation between instinct and drive. In the interim, before examining that *articulation*, we shall insist first on the analogy which exists, concerning our four "elements," between an instinct and a drive; or rather, in other words, we shall underscore the generality of the definitions of impetus, object, aim, and source, a generality which allows them to be applied to *both* instincts and drives. Such is, I believe, the wager implicit in "Instincts and Their Vicissitudes," and such as well is the trap that text sets for the unprepared reader: the essay would examine drives *in general*, not simply sexual drives but all those "groups" of drives—including consequently the "ego-drives" or "self-preservative drives"—concerning which we shall shortly have to ask whether the name *drive* is in fact properly applied to them. To deal with every *Trieb* in general is necessarily to proceed in an abstract manner. To deal with drives in general is to biologize them, to subject them to an analysis which is *also* valid for so-called instinctual patterns of behavior. As evidence, one need but invoke the validity of such concepts in recent analyses in the fields of animal psychology or ethology. The research of contemporary animal psychologists, specifically in Lorenz's school, makes extensive use, even if reference is not regularly made to Freud, of concepts analogous to his; specifically, the notion of "impetus" is employed, since the *hydraulic model*, which is most often invoked by Freud to account for the economic factor, is expressly adopted by them. The notion of an object which would simultaneously be contingent and, from a certain point of view, specific is present in the notion of a perceptual constellation triggering a specific act, and capable of releasing a specific mechanism because it includes a series of determined traits. As is known, it is by the use of perceptual lures, whose different characteristics are made to vary, that certain of these triggers have been precisely defined. Finally, the notion of an *aim* is also present in ethological analysis in the form of a fixed behavioral pattern, a series of chain reactions ending in a permanent discharge of tension: a cycle which may stop at any particular stage if the succeeding triggering device is not present to provoke the corresponding mechanism.

Having insisted on the *general* value of Freud's definitions, a generality which includes both a negative aspect (since the definitions may appear abstract) but also a positive one (since these notions can be shown to coincide with those of a science as concretely empirical as ethology), we shall return to the *Three Essays*, and to their very first page, on which is found a succinct description of the "popular" conception of sexuality. The *Three Essays* begin:

> The fact of the existence of sexual needs in human beings and animals is expressed in biology by the assumption of a "sexual drive," on the analogy of the instinct of nutrition, that is, of hunger. Everyday language possesses no counterpart to the word "hunger," but science makes use of the word "libido" for that purpose.
>
> Popular opinion has quite definite ideas about the nature and characteristics of this sexual drive. It is generally understood to be absent in childhood, to set in at the time of puberty in connection with the process of coming to maturity and to be revealed in the manifestations of an irresistible attraction exercised by one sex upon the other; while its aim is presumed to be sexual union, or at all events actions leading in that direction.

This "popular" conception is, at the same time, a biologizing conception in which sexuality, the sexual *drive*, is conceived of on the model of an *instinct*, a response to a natural need whose paradigm is hunger (if we may be allowed at this point to make more systematic use than Freud of the conceptual pair drive-instinct). In the case of sexuality, this need would appear to be grounded in a process of maturation, a process of strictly internal origin, in which the physiological moment of puberty is determinant; it would thus be a behavioral sequence narrowly determined by its "source," with a fixed and quite precise "object," since sexuality would focus uniquely and in a manner predetermined for all eternity on the other sex; finally, its "aim" would be similarly fixed: "sexual union, or at all events actions leading in that direction." We should, then, insist on the fact that this "popular conception," which Freud summarizes here in order to expose it subsequently to his attack, coincides with an image which may seem scientific, in the sense of a science of life, an image which, in the last analysis, is perhaps quite valid, at least in domains *other* than that of human sexuality. If we return now to the organization of the *Three Essays*, we shall understand better how that organization is modeled, in its movement, on the very object of the work: the entire organization may be understood as a function of a certain "destruction" (perhaps in the sense of Hegel's *Aufhebung*) of this "popular"—but also biologizing—image of sexuality. There are three chapters, as we recalled earlier. The first is "Sexual Aberrations," and we might subtitle that first chapter "The Instinct Lost." The second chapter is entitled "Sexuality," and we elaborate: "The Genesis of Human Sexuality." Finally, the third chapter, "The Transformations of Puberty"; perhaps then, in a sense, the instinct regained? No doubt, but regained at a different level. Rather than *regained*, we would propose provisionally a formula such as "The Instinct Mimed."

We shall treat the first *Essay* only briefly, and in order to situate the second, which is the principal focus of this chapter. It presents us with a polemical, almost apologetic catalogue of sexual aberrations. At stake is an effort to destroy received notions of a *specific aim* and *specific object* through a description of perversions. It is a presentation, moreover, which is distinguished neither by its scientific rigor nor by the exhaustiveness of its explanations. There is no basis for seeking in the *Three Essays* the alpha—and certainly not the omega—of the psychoanalytic theory of the perversions. The crux for Freud is to show just how extended, almost universal, the field of perversions is, and how their existence demolishes any idea of a determined aim or object for human sexuality. Sexuality, one might say upon reading this first chapter, gives the appearance, in a so-called normal adult, of an instinct, but that is only the precarious result of a historical evolution which at every stage of its development may bifurcate differently, resulting in the strangest aberrations.

Our consideration of the second *Essay* will center on a passage which delineates the essence of the matter in that it redefines sexuality as a function of its infantile origins. I refer to the conclusion of a section entitled "The Manifestations of Infantile Sexuality":

> Our study of thumb-sucking or sensual sucking [taken as a model of oral sexuality] has already given us the three essential characteristics of an infantile sexual manifestation. At its origin it *attaches itself to [or props itself upon: entsteht in Anlehnung an]* one of the vital somatic functions; it has as yet no sexual object, and is thus *auto-erotic*; and its sexual aim is dominated by an *erotogenic zone*.

We should observe straightaway that these three characteristics are found in most erotic manifestations of childhood and that they even transcend in large measure the sexuality of the *age* of childhood, marking definitively the entirety of human sexuality. The definition invokes three original and complex notions: the notion of *propping*, the notion of *auto-erotism*; finally, the notion of an *erotogenic zone*.

Propping [Etayage], the French reader will perhaps be surprised to hear, is a fundamental term in Freud's conceptual apparatus. In current translations of Freud, in French as well as in the excellent Standard Edition in English, the only trace of the Freudian concept is the sporadic and poorly justified use of an adjective derived from the Greek: "anaclitic." A prolonged consideration of Freudian terminology and an effort at retranslating Freud's work have led us to choose, along with the original French translator who had already used it unsystematically, the term *etayage (propping)* and its derivatives. If we have adopted that term, it is because it was necessary to bring into focus, as had not been done before, the rigorous conceptual value which the German word *Anlehnung*—meaning "to find support" or propping in something else—takes on in Freud. We have attempted thereby to bring into relief with its various resonances a notion long obscured by translations more concerned with elegance than rigor, specifically by an excessively learned and insufficiently explicit pseudoscientific term: *anaclisis*. In addition, the adjective *anaclitic* had in turn been inflected by an elaborate psychoanalytic tradition originating in a point which is already, in fact, secondary. For the term *anaclitic* was introduced by the translators in a text later than the *Three Essays*, the essay "On Narcissism" (1914), in which Freud contrasts two types of "object choice," two ways in which the human subject selects his love object in his own image, and an "anaclitic" object choice (*Anlehnungstypus*, in the German) in which (such at least is how the matter was a bit hastily interpreted) one's sexuality is based on the object of the function of self-preservation. Thus the term *propping* has been understood in this tradition as a leaning on the *object*, and ultimately a *leaning on the mother*. It may thus be intuited how an elaborate theory of a relation with the mother has come to inflect a notion intended to account for sexuality in its emergence. In fact, if one examines that notion more closely, one sees that originally it by no means designates a leaning of the subject on the object (of child on mother), even if such "leaning" is observable elsewhere. The phenomenon Freud describes is a leaning *of the drive*, the fact that emergent sexuality attaches itself to and is propped upon another process which is both similar and profoundly divergent: the sexual drive is propped upon a nonsexual, vital function or, as Freud formulates it in terms which defy all additional commentary, upon a "bodily function essential to life." It will thus be admitted that our divergence from Freud's thought is minimal, that we are in fact only rendering it more precise when we say that what is described as propping is a *leaning originally* of infantile sexuality on the instincts, if by instinct is meant that which orients the "bodily function essential to life"; in the particular case first analyzed by Freud, the instinct is hunger and the function feeding. Without the terminological coherence of Freud's writings being absolutely systematic, we shall nevertheless find, in a manner sufficiently motivated to allow us in turn to "lean" upon it, that the terms *function*, *need*, and *instinct* characterize generally the vital register of self-preservation in opposition to the sexual register.

With the *propping of the drive on the function*, we are faced not with an abstract genesis, a quasi-metaphysical deduction, but with a process that is described with the utmost precision in the archetypal example of orality. In orality, it is shown, two phases may be delineated: one consisting in sucking of the breast, and a second, quite different from the first, which is characterized as "sensual sucking." In the first phase—breast-sucking for nourishment—we are faced with a function or, to recall our earlier distinction, with a total instinctual pattern of behavior, one which is, in fact, so complete, as we have seen, that it is precisely hunger, the feeding pattern, which the "popular conception" assumes to be the *model of every instinct*. It is an instinctual pattern with its "impetus," and this time we should be able to specify precisely what may be hidden behind the energetic *x* term and, drawing on psychophysiology, to relate to a specific humoral or tissual imbalance that state of tension corresponding subjectively to the impression of hunger. We thus have an "impetus," an accumulation of tensions; a "source" as well, the digesive system, with—to localize and restrict things further—those points in which appetite is most specifically felt. A specific "object" is similarly introduced into the discussion. Shall we identify it as the breast? Well, no, since it is not the breast which procures satisfaction but the nourishment: milk. Finally, there is a preformed process or "aim," that process of breast-sucking which observers have undertaken to describe with great precision: the search for the nipple, feeding, the release of tension, pacification.

Now the crucial point is that simultaneous with the feeding function's achievement of satisfaction in nourishment, a sexual process begins to appear. Parallel with feeding there is a stimulation of lips and tongue by the nipple and the flow of warm milk. This stimulation is initially modeled on the function, so that between the two, it is at first barely possible to distinguish a difference. The object? It would appear to be furnished at the level of the function. Can we be sure whether it is still the milk or already the breast? The source? It too is determined by the feeding process, since lips are also part of the digestive system. The aim as well is quite close to the aim of nourishment. Ultimately object, aim, and source are intimately entwined in an extremely simple proposition allowing us to describe the process: "It's coming in by the mouth." "It" is the object; "coming in" is the aim, and whether a sexual or an alimentary aim is in question, the process is in any event a "coming in"; "by the mouth": at the level of the source, we find the same duplicity: the mouth is simultaneously a sexual organ and an organ of the feeding function.

Thus the "propping" consists initially in that support which emergent sexuality finds in a function linked to the preservation of life. We can find no better conclusion than the following quotation of another passage Freud devotes to the oral-erotic activity of the child:

> It is also easy to guess the occasions on which the child had his first experiences of the pleasure which he is now striving to renew. It was the child's first and most vital activity, his sucking at his mother's breast, or at substitutes for it, that must have familiarized him with this pleasure. The child's lips, in our view, behave like an *erotogenic zone*, and no doubt stimulation by the warm flow of milk is the cause of the pleasurable sensation. The satisfaction of the erotogenic zone is associated, in the first instance, with the satisfaction of the need for nourishment. To begin with, sexual activity attaches itself to [props itself upon] functions serving the purpose of self-preservation and does not become independent of them until later. No one who has seen a baby sinking back satiated from the breast and falling asleep with flushed cheeks and a blissful smile can escape the reflection that this picture persists as a prototype of the expression of sexual satisfaction in later life. The need for repeating the sexual satisfaction now becomes detached from the need for taking nourishment.

In the very act of feeding, the process of propping may be revealed in a culminating satisfaction that already resembles orgasm; but above all, in an immediately subsequent phase, we witness a separation of the two, since sexuality, at first entirely grounded in the function, is simultaneously entirely *in the movement which disassociates it* from the vital function. In fact, the prototype of oral sexuality is not in the sucking of the breast, and is not, in all its generality, the activity of sucking [*succion*] but rather what Freud, drawing on the works of Lindner, calls *das Ludeln oder Lutschen* [*suçotement*]. Henceforth, the object is abandoned, the aim and the source also take on autonomy in relation to the activity of feeding and the digestive system. With "sensual sucking" we thus come to the second "characteristic" referred to above, which is also a "moment" intimately linked to the process of propping which precedes it: auto-erotism.

Auto-erotism: Freud borrows the term from the sexologists of his time, notably Havelock Ellis, but he brings to it a new import: He defines it essentially in terms of the absence of an object (*Objektlösigkeit*): "a sexual activity . . . not directed towards other people." Now that definition prompts us to indicate immediately that if the notion of auto-erotism will fulfill an extremely important function in Freud's thought, it will simultaneously lead to a major aberration in psychoanalytic thinking and, perhaps, to a certain aberration in the thought of Freud himself, concerning the "object" and primal absence of the object. In such a perspective the object would be generated as it were *ex nihilo*, by a stroke of some magic wand, from an initial state regarded as totally "objectless." The human individual must thus "open up" to his world—things as well as individuals— starting from what we are tempted to call a state of biological idealism, no doubt even more inconceivable than philosophical solipsism. Deriving an object from an objectless state seems so unpromising a theoretical task to certain analysts that they do not hesitate to affirm—in a reaction which is laudable in its intentions but which only leads to a different error—that *sexuality per se* has an object from the beginning. Such is the position of a psychoanalytic author like Balint who undertakes, with frequently attractive arguments, to demonstrate that a "primary object love" in the child exists, so successfully, in fact, that henceforth all psychoanalytic discussion concerning the object has been restricted to the following alternative: either a total absence of objects for the human being, or the presence from the beginning of a *sexual* object. What path shall we take to avoid this false impasse? The solution is indicated on several occasions, in passages corresponding to moments of particular lucidity in Freud's thought. If we say "particular lucidity," it is out of a sense that certain discoveries may be forgotten, eclipsed, or repressed by their author: there are clear examples in the case of Freud himself, and notably concerning the point under consideration.

The following is a crucial passage, located further on, in the third *Essay*, but which summarizes the theses of the second *Essay*:

> At a time at which the first beginnings of sexual satisfaction are still linked with the taking of nourishment [i.e., in the propping phase], the sexual instinct has a sexual object outside the infant's own body in the shape of his mother's breast. It is only later that he loses it, just at the time, perhaps, when he is able to form a total idea of the person to whom the organ that is giving him satisfaction belongs. As a rule the sexual drive then becomes auto-erotic [*auto-erotism is thus not the initial stage*], and not until the period of latency has been passed through is the original relation restored. There are thus good reasons why a child sucking at his mother's breast has become the prototype of every relation of love. The finding of an object is in fact a re-finding of it.

The text cited has an entirely different ring to it from that vast fable of autoerotism as a state of the primary and total absence of an object: a state which one leaves in order to *find* an object; autoerotism is, on the contrary, a second stage, the stage of the loss of the object. A loss of the "partial" object, it should be noted, since it is a loss of the breast which is being considered, and Freud introduces at this point the precious observation that perhaps the partial object is lost at the moment in which the total object—the mother as person—begins to emerge. But above all, if such a text is to be taken seriously, it means that *on the one hand there is from the beginning an object, but that on the other hand sexuality does not have, from the beginning, a real object.* It should be understood that the real object, milk, was the object of the function, which is virtually preordained to the world of satisfaction. Such is the real object which has been lost, but the object linked to the autoerotic turn, the breast—become a fantasmatic breast—is, for its part, the object of the sexual drive. Thus the sexual object is not identical to the object of the function, but is displaced in relation to it; they are in a relation of essential *contiguity* which leads us to slide almost indifferently from one to the other, from the milk to the breast as its symbol. "The finding of an object," Freud concludes in a formulation that has since become famous, "is in fact a refinding of it." We would elucidate this as follows: the object to be redis-covered is not the lost object, but its substitute by displacement; the lost object is the object of self-preservation, of hunger, and the object one seeks to refind in sexuality is an object displaced in relation to that first object. From this, of course, arises the impossibility of ultimately ever rediscovering the object, since the object which has been lost *is not the same* as that which is to be rediscovered. Therein lies the key to the essential "duplicity" situated at the very beginning of the sexual quest.

The sexual *aim* is, similarly, in a quite special position in relation to the aim of the feeding function; it is simultaneously the same and different. The aim of feeding was ingestion; in psychoanalysis, however, the term used is "incorporation." The terms may seem virtually identical, and yet there is a slight divergence between the two. With incorporation, the aim has become the scenario of a fantasy, a scenario borrowing from the function its register and its language, but adding to ingestion the various implications grouped under the term "cannibalism," with such meanings as: preserving within oneself, destroying, assimilating. Incorporation, moreover, extends inges-tion to an entire series of possible relations; ingestion is no longer limited to food, since one can conceive of incorporation occurring in other bodily systems than the digestive apparatus: reference is thus made in psychoanalysis to incorporation at the level of other bodily orifices, of the skin or even, for instance, of the eyes. To speak of a visual incorporation may allow for the interpretation of certain symptoms. Thus from the aim of the function to the sexual aim, a transition exists which may still be defined in terms of a certain kind of displacement: one which, this time, follows an analogical or meta-phorical line, and no longer an associative chain through contiguity.

Finally, before leaving the vicissitudes of the aim in the process of propping, we should note, alongside the fantasmatic scenario or activity (incorporation, in the case of orality), a second kind of aim, no doubt linked to the scenario but much more localized, much less "dialectical": that of a "pleasure taken on the spot," the sheer enjoyment of sensual sucking. Between the fantasmatic aim of incorporation and the far more local and far less subtle aim of stimulating the lips, there is necessarily a complex relation that we shall have to reexamine.

There remains the problem of the *source*. We noted earlier that this is perhaps the central question if what we are presently studying is indeed the *origin*, thus precisely *the source of sexuality*. It should be emphasized that this is not simply a word game, neither for us nor for Freud, since we encounter in the *Three Essays* two meanings of the word *source*, with a relation between the two we should do well to follow. In an initial stage, *source* is taken in the most concrete and local sense of the term: as an erotogenic zone (to continue with the example of orality, the labial zone stimulated by the passage of milk). It is as though a biological scheme existed which would secrete sexuality from certain predetermined zones, exactly as certain physiological setups give rise to the need for nourishment through certain local tensions; we thus find the idea of a source in a strictly physiological sense. But we find as well a second meaning of the term, which is at least as interesting, although simultaneously far more general. We pass progressively from the erotogenic zone, as a privileged *place* for stimulation, to a far more extended series of processes. Already in the text of the *Three Essays*, but even more as Freud's considera-tions expand through broader clinical experience, the capacity to be the point of departure of sexual stimulation is revealed to be by no means the privilege of those zones which are successively described as the *loci* of oral, anal, urethral, or genital sexuality. Indeed, it is not exclusively those well-localized zones with their cutaneo-mucous covering, but every cutaneous region which is capable of serving as point of departure for sexual stimulation. In a later stage of his thought, Freud will posit that the erotogenic (areas productive of sexual stimulation) includes not simply every cutaneous region, but every organ, including internal ones; in so doing, he drew on an interpre-tation of the symptoms of hypochondria. Then, generalizing still further, he is eventually led to the position that every function and, finally, every human activity can be erotogenic. We are drawing in this last observation on the chapter in the *Three Essays* dealing with "indirect sources" of sexuality in order to note this time that far from being simply a biochemical process *localizable* in an organ or in a collection of differentiated cells, the "source" of sexuality can be as general a process as the mechanical stimulation of the body in its entirety; take, for example, the rocking of an infant or the sexual stimulation that may result from rhythmic jolts, as in the course of a railroad trip; or the example of sexual stimulation linked to muscular activity, specifically to sports. Then, in a still vaster perspective, Freud comes to assert that intense intellectual effort can itself be a point of departure for sexual stimulation—a fact that the most ordinary clinical observation confirms. Such is also the case for such general processes as affects, notably "painful" affects; thus, a suddenly emergent state of anxiety will frequently trigger a sexual stimulation. We shall, moreover, in a subsequent discussion of masochism, have occasion to return to the painful affect as an "indirect source" of sexuality.

Freud's conclusion on the subject reads:

> Sexual excitation arises as a concomitant effect [we shall retain this term *Nebenwirkung*, "marginal effect,". for it defines the process of propping in its double movement of leaning, and then detachment or deviation] in the case of a great number of internal processes [mechanical stimulation, muscular activity, intellectual work, etc.] as soon as the intensity of those processes passes beyond certain quantitative limits. What we have called the component drives [*Partialtriebe, pulsions partielles*] of sexuality are either derived directly from these internal sources or are composed of elements both from those sources and from the erotogenic zones.

We thus see the priority accorded by Freud, not to the source in its strictly physiological sense, but to the source in its so-called "indirect" sense, as in an "internal source" which ultimately is nothing but the transcription of the sexual repercussions of anything occurring in the body beyond a certain quantitative threshold. The interest of this redefinition of the source lies in the fact that any function, any vital process, can "secrete" sexuality; any agitation may participate in it. Sexuality in its entirety is in the slight deviation, the *clinamen* from the function. It is in the *clinamen* insofar as the latter results in an autoerotic internalization.

What, then, is ultimately the source of the drive? In the present perspective, we may say that it is the *instinct* in its entirety. The entire instinct with its own "source," "impetus," "aim," and "object," as we have defined them; the instinct, kit and caboodle with its four factors, is in turn the source of a process which mimics, displaces, and denatures it: the drive. To that extent the erotogenic zone, the privileged somatic zone, is not quite a source in the same sense as one might speak of the somatic source of an instinct; it is, rather, defined as a point particularly exposed to the concomitant, or marginal, effect—the *Nebenwirkung*—we have just evoked.

We thus conclude an all too brief itinerary. We shall put aside a consideration of the third chapter of the *Three Essays* in favor of other topics, and characterize it simply as the moment of the instinct regained; regained, as in any rediscovery—we demonstrated as much above concerning the rediscovery of the object—as other than it was in the beginning, for the discovery is always a rediscovery of *something else*. Clearly, this phase is oedipal. We shall presently neglect this third stage in order to insist on what gives to the first two chapters their meaning, orientation and unity. Consider once more what they entail: to that end we shall use the term *perversion*, since that indeed is the focus of the first chapter, with the sexual aberrations of adults, as well as of the second with the notion of a "polymorphous perverse" child. We shall consider the term *perversion* and the kind of movement operative within its very concept. Perversion? The notion is commonly defined as a *deviation from instinct*, which presupposed a specific path and aim and implies the choice of a divergent path (in biology, and currently in the "human sciences," reference is often made to "deviants"). This is so clearly the case that a glance at any psychiatric textbook reveals that its authors admit a remarkable diversity of perversions, concerning the entirety of the field of "instincts" and according to the number and classification of the instincts they adopt; not only sexual perversions but also, and perhaps above all, perversions of the moral sense, of the social instincts, of the nutritive instinct, etc. In the *Three Essays*, on the contrary, Freud founds his notion of perversion strictly on the sexual perversions. Are we thus suggesting, since deviance is necessarily defined in relation to a norm, that Freud himself would rally to the notion of a sexual instinct? Moreover, the definition of a "sexual instinct" ultimately would consist only in a revised and improved version of the "popular conception." Such is not the case, for Freud's dialectic is more fundamental. The movement we sketched above, a movement of exposition which is simultaneously the movement of a system of thought and, in the last analysis, the movement of the thing itself, is that the *exception*—i.e., the perversion— ends up by *taking the rule along with it*. The exception, which should presuppose the existence of a definite instinct, a preexistent sexual function, with its well-defined norms of accomplishment; that exception ends up by undermining and destroying the very notion of a biological norm. The whole of sexuality, or at least the whole of infantile sexuality, ends up by becoming perversion.

What, then, is perverted, since we may no longer refer to a "sexual instinct," at least in the case of the small child? What is perverted is still the instinct, but it is as a vital function that it is perverted *by* sexuality. Thus the two notions discussed at the beginning of this chapter—instinct and drive— once more are seen to meet and separate. The drive properly speaking, in the only sense faithful to Freud's discovery, *is* sexuality. Now sexuality, in its entirety, in the human infant, lies in *a movement which deflects the instinct, metaphorizes its aim, displaces and internalizes its object, and concentrates its source on what is ultimately a minimal zone, the erotogenic zone.* Concerning that erotogenic zone, which we have barely discussed, we should indicate the interest we are inclined to attribute to it. It is a kind of breaking or turning point within the bodily envelope, since what is in question is above all sphincteral orifices: mouth, anus, etc. It is also a zone of exchange, since the principal biological exchanges are borne by it (the prime example is again feeding, but there are other exchanges as well). This zone of exchange is also a zone for care, namely the particular and attentive care provided by the mother. These zones, then, attract the first erotogenic maneuvers from the adult. An even more significant factor, if we introduce the subjectivity of the first "partner": these zones *focalize parental fantasies* and above all *maternal fantasies*, so that we may say, in what is barely a metaphor, that they are the points through which is *introduced into the child that alien internal entity* which is, properly speaking, *the sexual excitation.* It is this alien internal entity and its evolution within the human being which will be the object of our next study.

JACQUES DERRIDA

Coming into One's Own

KEEPING IT IN THE FAMILY

Despite the richness and novelty of the content brought forward in the second chapter of *Beyond the Pleasure Principle*, despite numerous marching orders and steps forward, not an inch of ground is gained: there is no decision and not the slightest progress in the question that concerns the speculator, the question of the PP as absolute master. Nevertheless, this chapter is often remembered as one of the most important, the most decisive of the essay—particularly because of the story of the wooden reel and the *fort/da*. And since the repetition compulsion is associated with the death drive and a repetition compulsion seems to dominate the episode of the wooden reel, some feel that they can connect this story to the discussion and even the proof of the existence of a death drive. It means they haven't *read* the text: the speculator retains nothing of this *fort/da*, at least not in his proof about something beyond the PP. He claims that he can still explain the *fort/da* completely in the domain and under the authority of the PP. And he actually succeeds in doing so. It is indeed the story of the PP that he tells us, an important moment in his own genealogy, but a moment of himself.

Not that this chapter is devoid of interest, nor that the anecdote about the wooden reel has no bearing. Quite to the contrary: perhaps its bearing is just not inscribed in the register of *proof*, whose most obvious string is held by the question of whether "we" psychoanalysts are right in *believing* in the absolute domination of the PP. Where, then, is the bearing of the wooden reel inscribed?

If we consider the argumentative framework of the chapter, we notice

Translated by James Hulbert. From *Psychoanalysis and The Question of the Text*, edited by G.H. Hartman. Copyright © 1978 by The English Institute. The Johns Hopkins University Press, 1978.

that something repeats itself, and this process of repetition must be identified not only in the content (the examples), the materials described and analyzed) but also in Freud's very writing, in the "steps" taken by his text, in what it does as well as in what it says, in its "acts" as much as in its "objects." What obviously repeats itself in this chapter is the movement of the speculator to reject, set aside, make disappear (fort), defer everything that seems to call the PP into question. He notes that it is not enough, that he must postpone the question. Then he summons back the hypothesis of something beyond the pleasure principle only to dismiss it again. The hypothesis returns only like something that has not really returned but has merely passed into the ghost of its presence.

Let's begin with the "normal" and "primeval": the child, in the typical activity that is attributed to him—play. It appears to be an activity wholly subjugated to the PP (and indeed we shall see that such is the case and that it is wholly under the surveillance of a PP that is, however, tormented or shaped by his/its silent other)—an activity, moreover, as independent as possible of the second principle, the PR.

And this is what I shall call the argument of the wooden reel: a legendary argument that is neither story nor history nor myth nor fiction. Nor is it the systematic elaboration of a theoretical proof. It is fragmentary, without conclusion, selective: rather an argument in the sense of an outline. And this legend is already too legendary, overloaded, obliterated. In the face of the immense literature whose investment [investissement; also "cathexis"] this legendary argument has attracted, I should like to undertake a partial and naive reading, as naive and spontaneous as possible.

Here for the first time in this book is a passage that appears to be autobiographical and even domestic. This fact is veiled, but all the more significant. Freud says that he was a witness—an interested witness— to the experiment. It took place in his family, though he does not mention this. We know from other sources that the interested witness was none other than the child's grandfather. Even if an experiment could ever be restricted to observation, the conditions as they are defined in this account were not those of an observation. The experimental conditions here, supposedly those of adequate observation ("It was more than a mere fleeting observation, for I lived under the same roof as the child and his parents" [p. 8]), guarantee the observation only by turning the observer into a participant. But what part did he play? Can he decide his part himself? Neither the question of objectivity nor any epistemological question in canonical form has the slightest pertinence, for the very good reason that this experiment and the account of it claim to be nothing less than a genealogy of objectivity in general. How, then, can they be judged by the tribunal whose founding they repeat? But, inversely, what right does anyone have to forbid a tribunal to judge the conditions under which it is established, or to judge the account that an interested witness, a participant, gives of that establishment? Especially if the witness shows every sign of being strangely busy: busy, for example, producing the institution of his desire, making it the start of his own genealogy, making the tribunal and the legal tradition his heritage, his to delegate, his legacy, *his own*.

The account that we have is first sifted, pruned, deliberately restricted. This discrimination is in part declared at the outset. The speculator, who does not say that he has actually started to speculate yet, admits that he did not wish to "include the whole field covered by these phenomena" (p. 8). He has retained only those traits that were pertinent from the economic point of view. "Economic": we can already translate by playing a little (play is not yet forbidden at this phase of the origin of everything, of the present, the object, language, work, earnestness, and so forth) but not gratuitously from the viewpoint of the *oikos* [literally, "house"], the law of the *oikos*, of that which is one's own as one's own household [*domestico-familial*], and even, as we shall see in the same way, as one's own house-of-mourning [*domestico-funéraire*]. The speculating grandfather justifies the accounts that he is giving and the discrimination that he openly performs in them, by referring to the economic point of view. It has thus far been neglected in the "different theories of children's play," and it constitutes the privileged starting point for *Beyond the Pleasure Principle*, for what the one who keeps or gives the accounts is in the process of doing, i.e., of writing.

> These theories attempt to discover the motives which lead children to play, but they fail to bring into the foreground the *economic* motive, the consideration of the yield of pleasure involved. Without wishing to include the whole field covered by these phenomena, I have been able, through a chance opportunity which presented itself, to throw some light upon the first game played by a little boy of one and a half and created by himself [*selbstgeschaffen*]. It was more than a mere fleeting observation, for I lived under the same roof as the child and his parents for some weeks, and it was some time before I discovered the meaning of the puzzling activity which he constantly repeated.

From this first paragraph of the account onward, a single trait characterizes the object of observation, the action of the game: repetition, repeated repetition [*das andauernd, wiederholte Tun*]. That's all. The other characteristic, "puzzling," doesn't describe anything: it is empty, but with an emptiness that calls out and that, like every puzzle, calls for a story.

You may say: wait, there is another descriptive trait in this first paragraph. The game, which constitutes the repetition of repetition, is "*selbstgeschaffen*," a game that the child brought about or let come about by himself or by itself, spontaneously, and it is the first of this sort. But none of this (spontaneity, self-production, the primeval quality of the first time) contributes any descriptive content that does not go back to the self-engendering of self-repetition: the heterotautology (the definition of the speculative in Hegel) of repeated repetition, of self-repetition, in its pure form, which will constitute the game.

There is repetition between pleasure and displeasure, repetition of a pleasure and a displeasure, whose (pleasant/unpleasant) content is not an external aid to repetition but an inner determination, the object of an analytical predication. The possibility of this analytical predication will gradually develop the hypothesis of a "drive" that is more primeval than the PP and independent of the PP. The PP will be surpassed, is already surpassed in advance, by the speculation that he/it incites and by his/its own repetition.

Superpose what the grandfather says his grandson does, with all the earnestness that befits an elder grandson named Ernst (the importance of being earnest)—but not Ernst Freud, for the movement of this genealogy passes by way of the daughter, who is also a wife, i.e., who perpetuates the race only by risking the name (I'll let you follow the rounds of this factor until its reaches all those women about whom it's hard to know whether they kept the movement without the name or lost the movement in order to keep, or because they had kept, the name; I advise only that in the question of the analytic "movement" as the genealogy of the son-in-law, you not forget Judaic law)—superpose what he says that his grandson does earnestly on what he is doing himself in saying so, in writing *Beyond the Pleasure Principle*, in playing so earnestly (in speculating) at writing it. For the speculative heterotautology of the thing is that that "beyond" is lodged in the repetition of repetition of the PP.

Superpose: *he* (the grandson of his grandfather, the grandfather of his grandson) repeats repetition compulsively, but it all never goes anywhere, never advances by a single step. He repeats an operation that consists of pretending to dispatch pleasure, the object of pleasure or the pleasure principle, represented here by the wooden reel that is supposed to represent the mother (and/or, we shall see, the father, in place of the son-in-law, the father as son-in-law *[le père en gendre]*, the other family name), to bring it back again and again. He pretends to dispatch the PP in order to make it return endlessly, in order to note that it comes back of its own accord and to conclude: it is always there—I am always there. *Da.* The PP retains total authority, has never been away.

In every detail we can see the superposition of the subsequent description of the *fort/da* (on the grandson's side of the house of Freud) with the description of the speculative game, itself so assiduous and so repetitive, of the grandfather in writing *Beyond the Pleasure Principle*. It's not, strictly speaking, a matter of superposition, nor of parallelism, nor of analogy, nor of coincidence. The necessity that links the two descriptions is of a different sort: we shall not find it easy to give a name to it, but it is clearly the main thing at stake for me in the sifting, interested reading that I am repeating here. Who summons whom to return in this double *fort/da* that couples in the same genealogical (and conjugal) writing both the story and the one who is telling it (the "earnest" grandson's game with the wooden reel and the grandfather's earnest speculation with the PP)?

This simple question, left unanswered, suggests that the description of the earnest game of Ernst, the elder grandson of the grandfather of psychoanalysis, no longer must be read *only* as a theoretical argument, a strictly theoretical speculation that tends to conclude that what we have here is the repetition compulsion *or* the death drive *or* simply an inner limit to the PP (you know that Freud, whatever his allies and his opponents on this issue have claimed, never comes to a definitive conclusion about this). Rather, the description of Ernst's game can also be read as an autobiography of Freud; not merely an auto-biography entrusting his life to his own more or less testamentary writing but a more or less living description of his own writing, of his way of writing *Beyond the Pleasure Principle* in particular. It is not merely a superposition or a tautological reversal or mirror—as would be the case if Freud wrote down what his descendants dictated and thus held the first pen, the pen that is always passed from hand to hand; if Freud made a return to Freud by the mediation of his grandson. The auto-biography of *writing* at once posits and deposes, in the same motion, the psychoanalytic movement. I'll wager that this double *fort/da* cooperates in initiating the cause of psychoanalysis, in setting in motion the psychoanalytic "movement," in being that movement. If there lingers in the astounding event of this cooperation the unanalyzed remnant of an unconscious, if this remnant shapes and constructs with its otherness the auto-biography of this testamentary writing, then I wager that it will be handed down blindly by the entire movement of the return to Freud. The remnant that silently shapes the scene of that cooperation is doubtless unreadable, but it defines the sole urgency, the sole interest, of what remains to be done.

I have never wished to overuse the abyss, nor above all the abyss structure *[mise en abyme]*. I have no strong belief in it, I distrust the confidence that it, at bottom, inspires, and I find it too representational to go far enough, not to *avoid* the very thing into which it pretends to plunge us. What does the appearance here of a certain *mise en abyme* open on, and close around? This appearance is not immediately apparent, but it must have played a secret role in the fascination that this little story of the reel exerts upon the reader—this anecdote that might have been thought banal, paltry, fragmented, told in passing and without the slightest bearing, if we are to believe the very man who reports it. Yet the story that he reports seems to place the writing of the report into an abyss structure: what is reported has a bearing on the one who reports it. The site of what is readable, as the origin of writing, is borne away. Nothing can be set down in writing any more. The value of repetition "*en abyme*" of Freud's writing is in a relationship of structural mimesis to the relationship between the PP and "his"/"its" death drive. Once again, this drive is not opposed to the PP, but it etches into the PP with a testamentary writing "*en abyme.*" Such is presumably the "movement," in the irreducible novelty of its repetition, in the utterly singular event of its double relationship.

If we were to simplify the question, it would become, for example, how can an auto-biographical writing, in the abyss of an unterminated self-analysis, give *its* birth to a world institution? And how does the interruption or the limit of the self-analysis, cooperating in rather than impeding the *mise en abyme*, reproduce its mark in the institutionalization of psychoanalysis, in such a way that the possibility of this re-mark does not cease to produce offspring, multiplying the progeny of its splits, conflicts, divisions, alliances, marriages, and verifications?

Such is the speculation that characterizes this auto-biography; but rather than simplify the question, this time we should approach the process from the other direction and stress its apparent premise: what is auto-biography if all its consequences (as I have just enumerated them) are thus possible? Remember, Freud, the first and thus the only one to have undertaken, if not defined, self-analysis, did not himself know what it was.

To move on in my reading, I now have need of an essential possibility that fortune, if that's the word for it, turned into an event: all auto-biographical speculation, insofar as it constitutes a legacy and the institution of a movement without limits, must take into account, at the very moment of speculation, the mortality of the legatees. As soon as there is mortality, then in principle death can come at any moment. Thus the speculator can survive the legatee, and this possibility is inscribed in the structure of the legacy, and even in the extreme case of self-analysis. Untimely death and the silent state of the legatee: this is one of the possibilities of what dictates and makes the writer write—even the one who seems not to have written, Socrates, or the one whose writing is supposed to duplicate discourse or *listening* (Freud and certain others). So one gives oneself one's own movement, inheriting from oneself: it's set up so that the ghost, at least, can always collect. All he has to do is to pronounce a name as the guarantee of a signature.

It happened to Freud and to certain others, but the fact that the event takes place on the stage of the world is not in itself enough to illustrate the possibility of its happening.

And what follows is not merely an example.

One daughter is silent. Unlike a daughter who would make use of her father's name and influence in a lengthy discourse about who inherits what, the silent daughter seems perhaps to say, "Here's why your father has the word." Not only "my father," but "your father." Her name is Sophie: Freud's daughter, Ernst's mother, whose death knell will sound soon enough in the text—soft and low, in a strange note added after the fact.

THE NAME GAME

I shall resume Freud's account precisely where I left it, without omitting anything. He insists that the child is normal, a necessary condition for a relevant experiment. He is a model child, and thus his intellectual development is marked by no unseemly precociousness. He gets along beautifully with everyone.

Especially with his mother.

(I leave it to you, following the pattern already elaborated, to relate the content of the story to the scene of its writing, here, for example, switching the places of the narrator and the main character, or the couple, Ernst and Sophie, the third one (the father/husband/son-in-law) never being far away and sometimes even too close. In a traditional story [récit classique], the narrator, the supposed observer, is not the same as the author. If it were not different in this case (since what we have here is not presented as literary fiction), it would be—it will be—necessary to go over the distinction again between the "I" of the narrator and the "I" of the author, adapting it to a new "metapsychological" topography.)

Ernst, I was saying, gets along well with everyone—especially his mother, since he didn't cry when she was away. She would leave him for hours. Why didn't he cry? Freud seems pleased and at the same time surprised, even sorry. In the very sentence in which he ascribes to excellence of character the fact that his grandson didn't cry for his daughter (his mother) during such long absences, he adds "obwohl" ("even though"), even though he was very much attached to her; she had not only nursed him but had also never had anyone else in to care for him. But this small anomaly is soon passed over: Freud never follows up on the "obwohl." Everything is fine, wonderful child, *but*. Here's the "but": this wonderful child had one disturbing habit. It's hard to see right off how Freud, at the end of the amazing description of it that he offers, can calmly conclude: "I eventually realized that it was a game."

The child was not at all precocious in his intellectual development. At the age of one and a half he could say only a few comprehensible words; he could also make use of a number of meaningful sounds that were intelligible to those around him. He was, however, on good terms with his parents and their one servant-girl, and he was praised for being a "good little boy." He did not disturb his parents at night, he conscientiously obeyed orders not to touch certain objects... and above all he never cried when his mother left him for hours, even though he was greatly attached to this mother, who had not only nursed him herself but had also looked after him without any outside help.

There seems to be no shadow to mar this scene, no "but." There are a "however" and an "even though," stabilizers, inner compensations that describe a situation in equilibrium. He was by no means precocious (to the contrary, if anything), *but* his relations with his parents were fine; he didn't cry when his mother walked out on him, *but* he was attached to her, and no wonder. Do I alone detect a suppressed accusation here? Freud cannot help making excuses for his daughter's son. So what does he have to reproach him for?

The big "but" comes right after all this, yet the word "but" does not appear. It is replaced by a "now" *(nun)*: "Now, this good little boy had on occasion a disturbing habit" (p. 8, translation modified). The good qualities (in spite of everything) of this fine boy, his normality, his calm, his ability to put up with that beloved daughter (mother), no tears, no fears—it's pretty clear that all this is going to cost something. Everything here is elaborately structured, bolstered, governed by a system of rules and compensations, an economy that will appear shortly in the form of a bad habit. And that bad habit makes it possible for him to bear what the "good" ones cost him: the boy is a speculator, too. What does he pay (what does he purchase) when he obeys the order not to touch "certain objects"? How does the PP negotiate between good habits and bad? The grandfather, father of the mother and of the daughter, deliberately chooses the descriptive traits. I can see him anxious, under pressure, like a playwright or director who must act a part in his own play. In preparing the play, he hastens to be sure that everything is in order, then rushes to get into his costume. This takes the form of a dogmatic authoritarianism, unexpected decisions, interrupted sentences, questions that go unanswered. The stage is set, the actor-playwright-producer has done everything himself, and the curtain is about to go up. But we don't know whether it rises *on* the scene or *in* the scene. Before any of the characters appear, there is a curtained bed. In essence, entering or leaving means passing by that curtain.

(I leave it to you to raise this curtain on all the other words and things—curtains, canvasses, veils, screens, hymens, umbrellas, etc.—that have concerned me for so long.)

> Now, this good little boy had on occasion a disturbing habit of taking any small objects he could get hold of and throwing them far away from him into a corner, under the bed, and so on, so that hunting for his toys and picking them up again [*das Zusammensuchen seines Spielzeuges*] was often no easy chore.

Gathering, collecting for the purpose of returning: this is what the grandfather calls work, a chore, and often a difficult one. On the other hand, scattering, sending things far away, he calls a game, playing, and the objects that are moved he calls toys, playthings, *Spielzeug*. The whole process is divided, not in a division of labor but in a division between work and play, between the child's play and the parents' (often difficult) work. Why does he scatter everything he gets hold of, and *who* is scattering, dispatching, *what*?

The wooden reel has yet to appear. In a certain sense, it will be merely an example of the operation that Freud has just described—but an exemplary example, occasioning a supplementary "observation" that will be decisive for Freud's interpretation. The child throws and retrieves, scatters and gathers, gives and takes all by himself: he combines scattering and gathering, the different roles, work and play, in one participant, it seems, and one object. This is what the grandfather calls "a game," when all the strings are brought together and held in one hand, with the parents needed neither as workers nor as players.

So far the *Spielzeug* in question has been a collective: all the toys, the unity of a dispersible multiplicity, which the parents' task is to gather up again and which the grandfather gathers together in a single word. This collective unity is the equipment for a game that can become *dislocated*: moved and fragmented or scattered. If the child parts with his *Spielzeug* as if with himself and for the purpose of being gathered up and put back together, it is because he, too, is a collective, and the reassembly of that collective can give rise to a whole new range of combinations. Everyone who plays or works at gathering up the pieces has a piece of the game. Not that Freud says so, but he will say, in one of the two notes I've mentioned, that what in the child's "game" appears and disappears does indeed include the child himself or his image. He is part of his *Spielzeug*.

The wooden reel is still to come, after this interpretative anticipation: as he threw all his *Spielzeug* far away,

> he gave vent to a loud, long-drawn-out "o-o-o-o," accompanied by an expression of interest and satisfaction. His mother and the observer were agreed in thinking that [*nach dem übereinstimmenden Urteil*] this was not a mere interjection but represented the German word "*fort*" ["gone"]. I eventually realized that it was a game and that the only use he made of any of his toys was to play "gone" [*fortsein*] with them.

Freud's intervention (I don't say the grandfather's but that of the one who narrates what was experienced by the observer, the one who finally realized that "it was a game"; there are at least three agencies or personae of the same "subject": the speculator-narrator, the observer, and the grandfather, who is never explicitly identified with the other two by the other two, and so forth)—Freud's intervention, I say, merits special attention. He says that as observer he also interpreted—and *named*. Now what he calls a game, rather than work (work being the chore of gathering up what has been scattered), is, paradoxically, the operation that consists in not playing with one's toys: he used the toys (we are told) only to play that he was sending them far away. The "game" thus consists in not playing with one's toys but making them serve another function, i.e., *Fortsein*. Such would be the deflection, redirection, or *teleological* purposiveness of this game. But teleology, purposiveness of *Fortsein*, in view of what, of whom? What and who are served by this utilization of what ordinarily presents itself as gratuitous or useless, i.e., play, a game? Perhaps this nongratuitousness brings not one *single* benefit, and perhaps not a *benefit*, and perhaps not to a single person or agent of speculation. There is a tele-ology of the operation that is being interpreted and a teleology of interpretation. And there is more than one interpreter: the grandfather (our observer), the speculator and father of psychoanalysis (our narrator), and then, linked to each of these, the woman whose judgment, we are told, corroborates and coincides with her father's interpretation to such an extent that they can be superposed.

This concurrence linking father and daughter in the interpertation of the "o-o-o-o" as "*fort*" is unusual in several ways. It is hard to imagine the scene in detail, or even to credit its existence. Still, Freud does tell us that the boy's mother and the observer have somehow come together to make the *same* judgment about the meaning of the sound that their son and grandson made in their presence, indeed *for* them. There's no telling what the source of such an identification is. But you can be sure that wherever it comes from, it links the three characters in what we must now more than ever call the *same* speculation. In secret, they have all named the same thing.

Freud never stops to wonder about the language into which he translates the *o/a*. To recognize in those sounds a semantic content linked to a specific language (a certain opposition of German words) and from there a semantic content that goes beyond that language (the interpretation of the child's behavior) is a process that requires complex theoretical procedures. We may suspect that the *o/a* is not restricted merely to a formal opposition of values, the content of which may vary freely. If this variation is restricted (as we must conclude from the fact—if it concerns us—that the father and the daughter and the mother find themselves united in the same semantic reading), then we can state the following hypothesis: there is a proper name involved in those sounds, whether we mean this figuratively (every signified whose signifier can neither vary nor be translated into another signifier without loss of significance, suggests a proper-name effect) or literally.

And what if this perfect concurrence in the judgment handed down (*Urteil*) were what the son, i.e., the grandson, was after, if it were moreover what he believed in without knowing, without wanting to believe it? The father is away, *fort*—that is, *one* of the two fathers, the father of the little boy. As for Sophie's father, the father of psychoanalysis, he's still there.

The wooden reel still has not appeared. Here it is, as the text continues:

> One day I made an observation which confirmed my view. The child had a wooden reel [*Holzspule*; French, *bobine en bois*] with a piece of string tied round it. It never occurred to him to pull it along the floor behind him, for instance, and play at its being a carriage [*Wagen mit ihr zu spielen*]. What he did was to hold the reel by the string and very skilfully throw it over the edge of his little curtained [or "veiled"] bed, so that it disappeared into it, at the same time uttering his meaningful "o-o-o-o." He then pulled the reel out of the bed again by the string and hailed its reappearance with a joyful "*da*" ["there"]. This, then, was the complete game—disappearance and return. As a rule one witnessed only its first act, which was repeated untiringly as a game in itself, though there is no doubt that the greater pleasure was attached to the second act.

At the end of this last sentence, there is a footnote to which we shall come in a moment.

"This, then," says Freud, "was the complete game." Which implies immediately: this, then, is the complete observation, and the complete interpretation, of that game. If the completeness were obvious and certain, would Freud insist upon it, would he point it out as if it were necessary to close that completeness in all haste? We suspect all the more that the object or its description is incomplete because (1) the scene is that of an endlessly repeated supplementation, as if it could never become complete, and so on, and (2) there is something like an incompleteness axiom in the structure of the writing scene, owing to the position of the speculator as an interested observer. Even if completeness were possible, it would never appear to such an "observer," nor could he declare it to be complete.

But these are generalities. They outline only the formal conditions for determinate incompleteness, the significant absence of some especially pertinent characteristic—either in the scene described or in the description or in the unconscious that links them, their common inherited unconscious, telecommunicated in accordance with the same teleology.

Freud says that the greater pleasure, although it is observed less directly, is the *Wiederkommen*, the return, the coming again. Yet what becomes itself again by coming again (like a ghost) must be dispatched once more, again and again, if the game is to be complete.

The game *is* complete, he says. Yet he seems surprised and indicates a definite regret that it never occurred to the good little boy to pull the reel behind him and play *Wagen* (carriage, car, train) with it. It's as if the speculator (whose phobia for railroads is well enough known to put us on the right track) would have played train himself with one of those "small objects." This is the first query, the first perplexity, of the father of the object or the grandfather of the subject, of the father of the daughter (the mother, Ernst's object) or of the grandfather of the little boy (Ernst as "subject" of the *fort/da*). Why doesn't he play train or car? Wouldn't that be more normal? If he had been playing in his grandson's place (thus with his daughter, since the reel represents her, as he says in the next paragraph), the (grand)father would have played train (please grant me all these parentheses—the (grand)father, the daughter (mother)—they are necessary to indicate the blurred syntax of the genealogical scene, the fact that all the places are occupied, and the ultimate origin of what I have called the athetic nature [*l'athèse*] of *Beyond the Pleasure Principle*); and since the game is in earnest, it would then have been even more so, he says earnestly, but it never occurred to Ernst. Instead of playing on the ground, Ernst insisted on bringing the bed into the game, on playing with the thing over the bed but also in the bed. (Contrary to what many readers have gathered from the text and its translation, the child is not in the bed, it seems, when he throws the reel.) From outside the bed he throws the reel over the edge of the bed, over the veils or curtains that surround the edge; he pulls the car "out of the bed" to bring it back—*da*. Thus the bed is *fort*, which contradicts, perhaps, all desire.

What is playing train, for the (grand)father? Speculating: it would be never throwing the thing (but does the child ever throw it without having it on a string?), keeping it constantly at a distance, but the same distance (since the length of the string is constant), making or letting it move at the same time and with the same rhythm as oneself. This train never even has to return, for it never really leaves. The speculating grandfather makes sure of [*assure*; also "insures"] the thing only by depriving himself of a supplementary pleasure, the very one that he describes as the main one for Ernst, i.e., the second act, the return. He deprives himself of it to spare himself the pain or risk of the wager. And so as not to bring the desired bed into play.

If the child is indeed outside the bed but near it, concerned with the bed, which his grandfather seems to reproach him for, then the curtains, the veils, the fabric that hides the bars, do form the inner partition of the *fort/da*, the double screen that divides the *fort/da* on the inside, with its inner and outer faces, but only by gathering it with itself, pricking it twice, to itself— *fort:da*. This I call the *hymen* of the *fort:da*. The veil is the interesting thing about the bed and the *fort:da* of all these generations.

The grandfather regrets that his grandson never had these ideas (wise or crazy) of a game without a bed, but they didn't fail to occur to *him*. He even finds them natural, just the thing to improve the description, if not the game. In the same way, we might say, he regrets that his grandson did have the ideas that he had for him.

Was this bed, finally, with its so very necessary and so very indeterminate edge, a *couch*? Not quite, despite all the Orphism of speculation. And yet . . .

What the speculating (grand)father calls the complete game would be the game in the duality of its two phases: disappearing and coming back, absence and re-presentation. What links the game to itself is the *re-* of the return, the extra turn of repetition and reappearing. He insists that the greater quantity of pleasure is attached to the second phase, to the *re*-turn that determines everything, and without which nothing would come about. This permits us to anticipate that this operation, in its so-called "complete" totality, will come entirely under the authority of the PP. Far from being thwarted by repetition, the PP will also seek to recall in the repetition of appearing, of presence, of a repetition, as we shall see, that is mastered and that verifies and confirms the mastery that constitutes it (that of the PP). The mastery of the PP is none other than mastery in general; rather than the *Herrschaft* ["mastery"] of the PP, there is simply *Herrschaft* that *leaves* itself only to reappropriate itself, to *come* into its own (self)—a tautoteleology that, however, makes or lets the other return as his/its household ghost. It is thus predictable. What returns comes neither to contradict nor to oppose the PP but to erode it/him as its/his own other *[étranger]*, to hollow out an abyss in the PP, starting from a primevalness more primeval than the PP and independent of it/him, older yet in it/him: not, under the name of death drive or repetition compulsion, *another master* or an *antimaster* [contre-maître; cf. *contremaître*, "overseer"] but something other than mastery, entirely different. But whereas it is entirely different, it must not oppose, must not enter into a dialectical relationship with the master (life, the PP *as* life, living, alive), e.g., a master-slave dialectic. Nor must this non-mastery enter into a dialectical relationship with death, e.g., to become, as in speculative idealism, the "true master."

I do indeed say, the PP as mastery in general. At this point in our discussion, the supposed "complete game" no longer involves this or that specific object, e.g., the wooden reel or what it replaces. What's involved is the *re-* in general, returning in general, and disappearance/reappearance; not some object that goes out and comes back but the very going and returning, in other words the self-presentation of re-presentation, the self-returning of returning. This happens also to the object that becomes again the subject of the *fort:da*, the disappearance and reappearance of *oneself*, the object coming back into *his own*, himself.

And thus we come to the first of the two footnotes. It is a note to "the second act," to which "the greater pleasure" is said to be undoubtedly attached. What does the note say? That the child stages the usefulness of the *fort:da* with something that is no longer an object-object, an extra reel *[bobine]* replacing something else, but with a replacement *bobine* for the replacement *bobine*, with his own *bobine* ["noggin"], with himself as subject-object in the mirror and without the mirror. Here is the note:

> A further observation subsequently confirmed this interpretation fully. One day the child's mother had been away for several hours and on her return was met with the words "Baby o-o-o-o!" which was at first incomprehensible. It soon turned out, however, that during this long period of solitude the child had found a method of making *himself* disappear. He had discovered his reflection in a full-length mirror which did not quite reach to the ground, so that by crouching down he could make his mirror-image "gone" *[fort]*.

The child identifies with the mother, because he disappears like her and makes her return along with himself, by making himself return without making anything else return but himself, her in him(her)self. This he manages while remaining in the closest proximity to the PP; the PP never leaves, and it/he gives (gets) the greatest pleasure at this moment. He makes himself disappear, he masters himself symbolically, and he makes himself reappear from then on without the mirror, in his very disappearance, keeping himself (like his mother) on a string, on the wire. He makes himself *re-*, still in accordance with the law of the PP, in the grand speculation of a PP that seems never to leave him/itself, nor anyone. This recalling, by telephone or teletype [i.e., voice or writing, from afar], produces the "movement" by contracting itself, by signing a contract with itself.

HAROLD BLOOM

Freud's Concepts of Defense and the Poetic Will

A person tropes in order to tell many-colored rather than white lies to himself. The same person utilizes the fantasies or mechanisms of defense in order to ward off unpleasant truths concerning dangers from within, so that he sees only what Freud called an imperfect and travestied picture of the id. Troping and defending may be much the same process, which is hardly a comfort if we then are compelled to think that tropes, like defenses, are necessarily infantilisms, travesties that substitute for more truly mature perceptions. The potential power of trope necessarily dismisses all such pseudo-compulsion. Yet the analytical tendency in any lover of poetry ought to keep him vulnerable to the audacity of the wit of Thomas Love Peacock, who in *The Four Ages of Poetry* saw poetic trope as a "wallowing in the rubbish of departed ignorance, and raking up the ashes of dead savages to find gewgaws and rattles for the grown babies of the age." Defense in poetry then called up Shelley's reply, *A Defense of Poetry*, where amid so much magnificence, Shelley gave us the finest trope of critical transumption (or troping upon a previous trope) that I know. Speaking of the errors and sins of the men who were the great poets, Shelley grandly adds: "they have been washed in the blood of the mediator and redeemer, time." The reader is thus reminded that the infantilism of the grown baby is of that sort of which Shelley leaps, transcending Christian tropes of salvation and subtly recalling a marvelous figuration by the dark Heraclitus:

Time is a child playing draughts; the lordship is to the child.

If that is infantilism, then we need not fear a yielding to it. But clearly it is something else, something we want to call poetry, and to whose defense we spring. To defend poetry, which is to say, to defend trope, in my judgment is to defend defense itself. And to discuss Freud's concepts of defense is to discuss also what in romantic or belated poetry is the poetic will itself, the ego of the poet not as man, but of the poet as poet. Freud's triumph, in an aesthetic rather than a scientific sense, is that the reverse seems more true also. To discuss the poetic will without referring to the ego's defenses is less and less interesting.

But I must begin by defining, as best I can, the poetic will, taking Nietzsche as inescapable point of origin. One day when Nietzsche's Zarathustra crosses over a bridge, he is surrounded by a crowd of cripples. A hunchback, with admirable irony, utters a great challenge to the prophet:

> You can heal the blind and make the lame walk; and from him who has too much behind him you could perhaps take away a little.

Zarathustra refuses, saying that to take away the hump from the hunchback is to rob him of his spirit. Yet in his meditation upon redemption that follows, Zarathustra transcends the hunchback's irony and proceeds to dream a great dream of the will. All of us have too much behind us, and the prophet, though poignantly calling himself "a cripple at this bridge," gives us a vision of the will's limits and of the will's desire beyond limits:

> To redeem those who lived in the past and to re-create all "it was" into a "thus I willed it"—that alone should I call redemption. Will—that is the name of the liberator and joy-bringer; thus I taught you, my friend. But now learn this too: the will itself is still a prisoner. Willing liberates; but what is it that puts even the liberator himself in fetters? "It was"—that is the name of the will's gnashing of teeth and the most secret melancholy. Powerless against what has been done, he is an angry spectator of all that is past. The will cannot will backwards; and that he cannot break time and time's covetousness, that is the will's loneliest melancholy.

A little further on, Zarathustra sums up this wisdom for us:

> This, indeed this alone, is what *revenge* is: the will's resentment against time and time's "it was."

Nietzsche does not mean that this will is itself the poetic or creative will, but the burden here must be taken on by the poet above all persons, since earlier in the Second Part *Zarathustra* Nietzsche twice attacks the poets, meaning Goethe in particular. In the rhapsody "Upon the Blessed Isles," we are warned that the poets lie too much, and yet the creative will is exalted. Out of the poets, if they cease to lie, will come "ascetics of the spirit," as Zarathustra will prophesy later.

But *can* they cease to lie, and particularly *against* time's "it was"? What is the poetic drive, or instinct to make what can reverse time? Freud ended with a vision of two drives, death drive and Eros or sexual drive, but he posited only a single energy, libido. The poetic drive or will is neither masked death drive nor sublimated sexual drive, and yet I would not assert for it a status alongside the two Freudian drives. Instead I will suggest that the creative will or poetic drive puts the Freudian drives into question, by showing that those drives themselves are defenses, or are so contaminated by defenses as to be indistinguishable from the resistances they supposedly provoke.

It isn't possible to ask coherently what Freud meant to mean by "defense" without deciding first what he meant to mean by a "drive" (*Trieb*). The drive or urge (setting aside the weak translation "instinct") is a dynamic movement that puts pressure upon a person towards some object. Your body and mind are stimulated, whether sexually and towards self-preservation, or towards aggression and death, and your body and mind therefore become tense. This tension needs resolution, and so the drive or urge moves upon some object so as to end tension. That Freud cannot be talking about merely biological impulses always should have been clear, long before the drives became overtly cosmological and hence mythological in *Beyond the Pleasure Principle*. Freud postulates that the psyche indeed has bodily intentions, or as he finally put it in his *Outline of Psychoanalysis*, drives are "the somatic demands upon mental life." Since psyche and body are conceived as a radical dualism, Freud is justified in seeing the drive as a frontier concept, neither truly mental nor truly physical. "Drive" is thus a dialectical term. Philip Rieff expressed this nicely when he wrote that the drive, to Freud, is "just that element which makes any response inadequate." A dialectical concept necessarily is subject to "vicissitudes," and if it invokes the will, we can be sure that a shadow or blocking-agent will threaten the will, that anteriority will make a stand against desire.

Yet defense, in Freud, is a far less mythological concept than the drive, and also is less dialectical. No one has ever demonstrated to us that drives even exist, but no hour of our lives goes by without reminding us painfully that the entire range of defense mechanisms can be at work unceasingly. Jacques Lacan has insisted that the four fundamental concepts of psychoanalysis are the unconscious, the compulsion to repeat, the transference, and the drive. I am not a psychoanalyst, but as an amateur speculator I would ask whether defense is not *the* most fundamental concept of psychoanalysis, and also the most empirically grounded of all Freud's path-breaking ideas? Repression is the center of Freud's vision of man, and when a revised theory of defense broke open the white light of repression into the multicolored auras of the whole range of defenses, then Freud had perfected an instrument that even psychoanalysis scarcely has begun to exploit. The theory of defense is now essentially where Freud left it, and it seems to me startling that ego psychology should have done so little to develop what might have been its main resource. Yet it may be inevitable that so agonistic a concept as defense should make Freud's followers wary of entering upon a struggle in which the Founder is doomed always to win.

Freud's earliest notion of defense was very simple; defense was what put an idea out of the range of consciousness. But even that simple a concept is a trope, since the flight or distancing of an idea, putting it out of range, is hardly literal language (whatever *that* may be). And though this first concept of defense was intellectually simple, its figuration was very complex. A sustained meditation upon Freud's rhetoric would have to engage the highly problematic troping of flight as the prime image of repression throughout his work, a troping that he shares with Milton, whether we think of Satan exploring the abyss, Eve's dream of flight, or Milton's own stance in his invocations.

Why Freud, in 1894, chose the word *Abwehr* for this most crucial of all his concepts I do not know, but the choice was in some respects a misleading one. Freud's *Abwehr* is set against *change*; it is in the first place then a stabilizing mechanism. Defense, in war or in sport, seeks more than stability; it seeks victory, or the annihilation of change. Perhaps Freud selected the word *Abwehr* because he intuited even then, back in 1894, that the ego's pleasure in defense was both active and passive, and so an ambiguous concept of ego required a more ambiguous process than mere stabilization in its operations against internal excitations.

Defense, though it be against drive, in actuality works against representations of the drive, and these can be only fantasies, memories, signals, unless a particular situation is interpreted by the ego as fantasy or signal. But defense is so contaminated by drive that defense also becomes fantasy or signal. I merely state the clinical evidence that everyone encounters every day, but this leads to the particular difficulty or inadequacy of Freud's concepts of defense, both early and late. Defense is unique among all central Freudian formulations in that its weaknesses are entirely theoretical, and not at all practical or empirical. Why is there psychic defense anyway? Why should an urge arising from the drive cause unpleasure to any ego whatsoever? I do not believe that Freud ever found a single clear answer to these questions. Later I will suggest that this failing is what compelled Freud to his mythological speculations in *Beyond the Pleasure Principle*.

Defense, for poets, always has been trope, and always has been directed against prior tropes. Drive, for poets, is the urge for immortality, and can be called the largest of all poetic tropes, since it makes even of death, literal death, our death, a figuration rather than a reality. But here I return to the problematic of the poetic will, in order to explore that analogue of the mutual contamination of drive and defense in the Freudian vision.

Following Nietzsche, I have suggested that the poetic will is an argument against time, revengefully seeking to substitute "It is" for "It was." Yet this argument always splits in two, because the poetic will needs to make another outrageous substitution, of "I am" for "It is." Both parts of the argument are quests for priority, and Freud takes his place in a tradition that goes from Vico to Emerson and Nietzsche whenever the founder of psychoanalysis speculates upon priority, which is so frequent an undersong throughout his writings.

The *psyche*, the image or trope of the self, has an invariable priority, for Freud, over reality or the object-world. Rieff expresses this rhetorical priority of mind over reality in Freud by returning us to the most fundamental of Western synecdoches, man as microcosm and the cosmos as macrocosm: "The self was no alien from the natural world; we were conscious of being not only subjects but objects of nature among other natural objects." The dominant influence upon Freud, here as elsewhere, as noted by so many exegetes from Rank to Rieff, is certainly Schopenhauer, a presence difficult to evade in Freud's Vienna.

Schopenhauer's account of repression emphasized only the derangements of memory, but in his theory of the Sublime the philosopher more authentically can be judged Freud's precursor. If we substitute for Schopenhauer's conscious turning-away Freud's unconsciously purposeful forgetting, then Schopenhauer's story of how the will is made poetic and Sublime becomes Freud's story of repression:

> . . . But these very objects, whose significant forms invite us to a pure contemplation of them, may have a hostile relation to the human will in general, as manifested in its objectivity, the human body. They may be opposed to it; they may threaten it by their might that eliminates all resistance, or their immeasurable greatness may reduce it to nought. Nevertheless, the beholder may not direct his attention to this relation to his will which is so pressing and hostile, but, although he perceives and acknowledges it, he may consciously turn away from it, forcibly tear himself from his will and its relations, and, giving himself entirely up to knowledge, may quietly contemplate, as pure, will-less subject of knowing, those very objects so terrible to the will . . . he is then filled with the feeling of the *sublime*. . . .

Repression, like the movement to the Sublime, is a turning operation, away from the drive and towards the heaping up of the unconscious. Pragmatically repression, like Schopenhauer's Sublime, exalts mind over reality, over the hostile object-world, though in Freud's valorization this exaltation is highly dialectical. The unconscious mind is rhetorically an oxymoron, and the augmentation of the unconscious, though it cuts away much of the domain of the object-world, is covertly a parody version of Schopenhauer's contemplation.

I have been following a circuitous path to a declaration that the poetic will, or urge to the Sublime, is just as mythological an entity, no more and no less, as libido or the death-drive. The chiasmus that Laplanche isolates as the rhetorical figure for the relation of Eros to Thanatos appears again in the relation of trope to the poetic will. Freud's concepts of defense are themselves drives, and his difficult notion of the drive itself is a defense. Against what? Lacan, in his lecture *The Deconstruction of the Drive*, calls the drive a fundamental fiction, in Bentham's sense of a "fiction," and so Lacan is able to speak of a constant force, beyond biology: "It has no day or night, no spring or autumn, no rise and fall." Lacan even speaks of the drive as *montage*, meaning that every drive must be partial, and also that the scopic drive becomes the true model for understanding. As Lacan says, in one of his superb breakthroughs: "What one looks at is what cannot be seen." Drive is ambiguous, a synecdoche for that aspect of every ego "who, alternately, reveals himself and conceals himself by means of the pulsation of the unconscious." Whatever Lacan intends here, I read him as interpreting the Freudian synecdoche as being at once the partial drive and its defensive vicissitudes. Drive therefore defends against its own incompleteness, its own need to look at what cannot be seen.

But perhaps what Freud always defended against, until *Beyond the Pleasure Principle*, was the possibility that a monistic vision of human aggression would crowd out the dualistic vision of human sexuality. If this speculation were wholly correct, then the mythology of drives was a perpetual defense against a Nietzschean nihilism, against seeing the will to power as the true center of mankind. It seems clear today that the full range of defenses elaborated by Anna Freud are perfectly coherent entities in the context of aggression, without any necessary recourse to sexual neuroses. As I read the great epilogue-essay *Analysis Terminable and Interminable*, it is Freud's belated valorization of the castration complex, a final attempt to give the theory of sexuality equal privilege with the theory of aggressivity's valorization of the death drive.

Freud, in my judgment, wrote two texts which truly are High Romantic crisis-poems, *On Narcissism: An Introduction* and *Beyond the Pleasure Principle*. I am going to give a full reading here only to the latter, strictly following the paradigm of the crisis-lyric as I have developed it in some previous books. But to account for the full range of psychic tropes or verbal defenses in *Beyond the Pleasure Principle*, and to illustrate further the mutual contamination of the concepts of drive and defense in Freud, I turn first to the essay, really the prose rhapsody, on narcissism. Though I will dissent implicitly from much that Laplanche says, my reading of this essay is indebted to the fourth chapter of *Life and Death in Psychoanalysis*. The binary rhetoric of Lacan and Laplanche, with its reductive reliance upon Jakobson's metaphor/metonymy pseudo-dialectic, accounts for my principal unhappiness with the "French reading" of Freud, but that is an argument to be conducted elsewhere.

The concept of narcissism, as we ought never to forget, was the actual engine of change in Freud's theory. In the crisis-year of 1914, Freud's theory at first seemed complete, but the vehement burst of inspiration in Rome, during "seventeen delicious days" with Minna Bernays, changed all that. If Minna was the Muse, the Sublime antagonist was the treacherous Gentile son, Jung, whose appropriation of Freud's earlier version of the ego helped provoke a severe *clinamen* away from that ego. The earlier ego was a kind of Virgilian *logos*, dependent upon repression of the drive, upon the tropological flight of images, memories, thoughts permeated by the ambivalences of drive. This ego is still vulnerable to the devastating critique of J. H. Van den Berg that "the theory of repression . . . is closely related to the thesis that there is sense in everything, which in turn implies that everything is past and there is nothing new. . . ." Van den Berg might well be criticizing Virgil, but not Ovid; and I would venture that the later Freudian ego, the narcissistic ego, is an Ovidian image. The simplistic conflict of drives—ego drives against sexual drives—is over, because the narcissistic ego is not at all an agent directing itself against a sexual drive, an Aeneas defending himself from a Dido of Carthage. From the ambiguous cosmos of the drive we have moved to an Ovidian flowing world of desire and wish, a cosmos where a more radical dualism lurks, the cosmos of Eros and Thanatos, as it will prove to be.

It is always worth recalling that Freud initially followed Ovid, in 1910, when he used the term "narcissism" for the first time, to refer to homosexuals taking themselves as their own sex object. In the wavering interplay between the ego-libido of self-preservation and object-love, Freud found a more powerful trope for his earlier balancings of the drive as taking place between mind and reality. Captivated by its own bodily image, the Ovidian ego confines libido within the flood-gates of the psychic microcosm, a confinement that allowed Lacan his prime heresy of the mirror-stage.

After 1920, with his second theory of the psyche, Freud was to espouse a more primal heresy, almost a Gnosis, in the absolute dualism that set against all object relations a primary narcissism, a true First Idea, glorying in priority, and solipsistically free of objects, as in Schopenhauer's Sublime. There is no distinction between id and ego, precursor and Ovidian poet, in the curiously sleep-like vision of primary narcissism. The Stevensian image of a child asleep in its own life is precisely applicable to Freud at this single moment. As in Whitman's *Song of Myself*, the distinction between autoeroticism and narcissism wavers and those two states of the psyche uneasily merge.

Lacan and Laplanche, in their different but complementary ways, have shown that Freud placed his concept of libido in a more coherent context after 1914 by hinting that psychic energy truly derives from the "narcissistic passion," and also that the essay on narcissism was able to tie together the two previously disjunctive notions of psychic topography and the theory of drives. Laplanche brilliantly reads the essay's dialectic as: narcissism is a love of the self; narcissism is a love of the ego; this investment of self-love actually *constitutes* the otherwise elusive ego.

At the least, Lacan and Laplanche help explain why the breakthrough of the narcissism essay led Freud on to the writing of *Beyond the Pleasure Principle*. The dialectics of aggression, so long evaded by Freud, follow the realization that narcissistic self-esteem, once badly wounded, must *defend* itself by aggression. Aggression rising up as a defense against the narcissistic scar that everyone suffers during infancy is still the most persuasive account we have for why human aggressivity develops so early. With this link between the theory of narcissism and the aggressive drive firmly kept in mind, I turn now to a full reading of *Beyond the Pleasure Principle*. A revisionary text like *Beyond* should be susceptible to an analysis on the scheme of my "revisionary ratios," if they are to be of any general use in reading difficult works that turn upon issues of crisis and catastrophe.

Beyond the Pleasure Principle is divided into seven chapters of which the last is very brief, and clearly serves as a coda. I will interpret the book here as a dialectical lyric, indeed as a post-Romantic crisis lyric. Such an interpretation must be willing to risk outrageousness. Jacques Derrida warns against any premature classification of *Beyond* as a literary text, but I intend to experiment with such a premature reading anyway. A text self-revisionist to this degree is almost definitive of one central stigma of the literary.

Freud's darkest precursor in *Beyond the Pleasure Principle* is necessarily himself, but Chapter I performs a double *clinamen*, an ironic swerve away both from the pre-1919 Freud and from the visions of Schopenhauer and Nietzsche. What looks like self-contradiction in Chapter I is an irony or allegory, in which Freud says one thing and means another. What he says is that the pleasure principle has priority over the principle of constancy. What he means is that the psychoanalyst need not base his speculations upon the empirical groundings of late-nineteenth-century biology and physics.

The concept of the pleasure principle never changed in Freud, but its hierarchical status in regard to other principles was always unstable. Evidently this resulted from the economic nature of the pleasure principle, which is defined dualistically as a drive that seeks to attain a reduction in the quantity of excitation, while fleeing any increase in such excitation. The reductive quest and the repressive flight are not tropes easily assimilated to one another. Something of a similar rhetorical difficulty appears in the images that define the principle of constancy. The psyche is described as maintaining the quantity of excitation in itself at as low and constant a level as can be achieved. But this level is reached by strikingly mixed images: excessive energy must be discharged, while any further augmentation of excitement must be evaded. If it cannot be evaded, then it must be repressed. Thus both principles—pleasure and constancy—require descriptions antithetical *in themselves but not to one another*. The rhetorical pattern of the two principles is much the same, which may be why Freud begins *Beyond* with the apparently self-contradictory notion that the constancy principle "is only another way of stating the pleasure principle." But Freud's own dominant trope here is an irony. Only the repressive element in the two principles verges upon an identity. The active element in the pleasure principle is a reductive nay-saying to every stimulus, but in the constancy principle it is an eruption, a volcanic release. By assigning priority to the negative, Freud prepares for his second topology, his final mapping of the mind. I suggest now that a defensive operation, a reaction-formation, is at work in Freud in this revisionary preparation, which culminates in *The Ego and the Id* (1923) and in *Inhibitions, Symptoms, and Anxiety* (1926). Anna Freud remarks that "reaction-formation secures the ego against the return of repressed impulses from within," and the repressed impulse here is nothing less than Freud's own scientism. I crave the indulgence here of quoting my own *A Map of Misreading*:

> . . . dialectical images of presence and absence, when manifested in a poem rather than a person, convey a saving atmosphere of freshness, however intense or bewildering the loss of meaning.

I would apply this to *Beyond the Pleasure Principle*'s first chapter by saying that its dialectical image of presence is the pleasure principle, and of absence the constancy principle. In order to break with his first topology, Freud will bewilder us by reorienting his dualisms. Against his own drive for scientific authority, he now swerves into a purely speculative authority. Against the dualism of Schopenhauer, which set up the Will or thing-in-itself in opposition to the objective world, the world as representation, Freud now opts for a more drastic dualism, or at least what he must have regarded as the most thoroughgoing of dualisms. Beyond the pleasure principle lies not the world as representation, but what Milton had called the universe of death.

Between the first two chapters of *Beyond*, Freud negotiates what I have called a Crossing of Election, a disjunctive awareness of his own revisionary crisis as founder of psychoanalysis. The crisis-question is not: "Am I still a psychoanalyst when I am at my most speculative?" but rather, "Is not psychoanalysis the only true mode of speculation?" To this question, the text of *Beyond* will render a triumphant and affirmative answer, whether or not the reader is prepared to yield to its authority. But this answer is deferred, and Chapter II instances a new defensive strategy. Freud's own playing-out of the vicissitudes of reversal and of turning against one's own self.

Not only is there a disjunctive gap between Chapters I and II, but Chapter II is highly disjunctive in itself. Its two subjects—traumatic neurosis and children's play—are not only antithetical in regard to one another, but Freud emphasizes their overt disjunction by his extremely abrupt and arbitrary transition between them. Their true connection is rhetorical, by way of Freud's highly characteristic synecdoche of neurosis as mutilated part, and psychic health as macrocosmic unity. Rieff has priority in having described this accurately as Freud's master trope. A neurotic's dream's are seen as belated efforts to master trauma *after* the shock has been inflicted. With the keenest element in his genius, which can be called nothing but uncanny, Freud intuits that the crux here is repetition, and in addition to the text of *Beyond*, made in 1921, he hints that masochism informs this repetition. Suddenly we are given the narrative concerning Freud's infant grandson, with his ingenious game of the "*fort-da.*" Whereas the neurotic repeated his trauma in nightmare, the healthy baby repeated a distressing experience as a game. Rhetorically, by synecdoche, traumatic nightmare is a failed game, because it lacks the joyful restitution of a "*da.*" But Freud does not make the rhetorical interpretation. Games *and* art, he says, are not his concern. In the higher speculation that is psychoanalysis, the quarry must be "the operation of tendencies *beyond* the pleasure principle, that is, of tendencies more primitive than it and independent of it."

In my reading, Chapter II is a *tessera*, an antithetical completion that fails to complete, and that leaves Freud exposed to the literary equivalent of the vicissitudes of drive, that is, to a certain cognitive and imagistic reversal that is self-wounding. The repetition-compulsion is itself a synecdoche for the wounded condition of Freud's earlier hypotheses when he confronts them in the post-war atmosphere of 1919. He had been repeating only a part of psychoanalysis, he now believes, under the delusion that he has mastered the whole of it. Tacitly, and perhaps unknowingly, his text lets us understand that his own earlier synecdoches were incomplete.

With Chapter III we have what I would call Freud's *kenosis*, an emptying-out of his prior stance (pre-1919) which manifests the one repetitive defense to which he was subject: isolation. Too strong a psyche to suffer regression or undoing, he nevertheless shares with the strongest poets the metonymic defense that burns away context. Isolation separates thoughts from all other thoughts, usually by destroying or injuring temporality. Even as we see Stevens, in *The Auroras of Autumn*, defend his poetic self by an undoing metonymnic movement, so in Chapter III we can observe Freud defending his psychoanalytic strength by isolating too rigorously a crucial element in his *praxis*: the transference. What is emptied out of its earlier, hoped-for fullness in Chapter III is precisely an idealized transference, and the first product of this *kenosis* is what Freud grimly calls a "fresh, 'transference neurosis.'" Something intense, which I surmise is his isolating compulsion to repeat, fixates Freud to the frustrating difficulties of transference throughout Chapter III. What ought to have been an exposition of repetition itself becomes an eloquent lament that repeats the noble sorrows of the analyst as he struggles on against the transference neurosis.

The frightening trope of the "narcissistic scar" conveys overtly the infant's first failure in sexual love. Does it covertly carry some sense of Freud's more exalted wound of triumph in his agon with all prior speculations, his own included? The "daemonic" power that psychoanalysis reduces as repetition-compulsion is cited by Freud as being present in what he calls the lives of normal people. Is he, Freud, the first listed of those "whose human relationships have the same outcome"? Whose career is it that is summed up in "the benefactor who is abandoned in anger after a time by each of his *protégés*, however much they may otherwise differ from one another, and who thus seems doomed to taste all the bitterness of ingratitude"?

It would seem then that it is the reign of the pleasure principle "over the course of the processes of excitation in mental life" that is truly emptied out in Chapter III. In Chapter 4 I interpreted Freud's use of Tasso here as an allegory of the founder's Sublime wounding of his fundamental concept of the drive. But nearly every paragraph in Chapter III voids something that Freud earlier had posited. Very much in the mode of the Sublime poet, Freud comes up to what I have called a Crossing of Solipsism in the gap between the end of Chapter III and the start of Chapter IV. The question becomes not the poetic one of the possibility of love for others, but the psychoanalytic one of affective investment (cathexis) in Freud's earlier self and its conceptualizations. Enormous strength flows in again with the *daemonizations* of Chapter IV, as Freud begins to open himself more fully to his own darkest and most powerful speculations.

Yet this is a strength of Freud's own repression, of his flight from vexing memories, indeed even from memories of Chapter I of the very book he is writing! Chapter IV is an indeliberate exercise in the Grotesque, with much of its rhetoric a curious litotes, and with its argument colored by images of depth. Freud represses his new freedom from scientism, and the repression allows a certain bathos its moment in the text:

> Let us picture a living organism in its most simplified possible form as an undifferentiated vesicle of a substance that is susceptible to stimulation. . . . This little fragment of living substance is suspended in the middle of an external world charged with the most powerful energies; and it would be killed by the stimulation emanating from these if it were not provided with a protective shield against stimuli. . . . *Protection against* stimuli is an almost more important function for the living organism than *reception of* stimuli. . . .

Supposedly owing this model to embryology, Freud actually owes it to his own defense against biologism, the biologism that consciously he embraced and never could bear to disavow. This grotesque organism is a kind of time-machine, because its "protective shield" precisely does the work of Nietzsche's revengeful will, substituting a temporality that does not destroy for one that would, if mortal time were not warded off. The repressed movement from scientism to speculation here achieves a curious triumph, and allows Freud to revise fully his views of dreams that occur in traumatic neuroses, or dreams recalling childhood traumas that rise during the course of a psychoanalysis. Here are the accents of rhetorical triumph as Freud acquires a new, more Sublime confidence in the fusion of his speculative powers and psychic realities:

> If there is a "beyond the pleasure principle" it is only consistent to grant that there was also a time before the purpose of dreams was the fulfillment of wishes. This would imply no denial of their later function. But if once this general rule has been broken, a further question arises. May not dreams which, with a view to the psychical binding of traumatic impressions, obey the compulsion to repeat—may not such dreams occur *outside* analysis as well? And the reply can only be a decided affirmative.

What fascinates me here is Freud's astonishing rhetorical authority. In response to so scrupulous, so knowing, so rational a voice, even the wariest reader must yield, though the reader yields only to the author's revisions and reversals of earlier formulations. It is fitting that Chapter V, which follows, should be a sublimation or *askesis* of the crucial and invariably problematic theory of the drives. *How*, Freud asks, is the predicate of being *Triebhaft* related to repetition-compulsion? The answer is a definition of drive that sublimates Freud's earlier account of drive, metaphorically substituting "drive" for the defenses of repetition: undoing, isolating, regressing:

> At this point we cannot escape a suspicion that we may have come upon the track of a universal attribute of drives and perhaps of organic life in general

which has not hitherto been clearly recognized. *It seems then, that a drive is an urge inherent in organic life to restore an earlier state of things* which the living entity has been obliged to abandon under the pressure of external disturbing forces....

Where once we encountered a drive only by embodying defenses against it, now we experience a drive as a regressive defense. But against what? Against life itself would seem to be the answer, or at least against animation. Drives are *détours*, in Freud's new metaphor, "circuitous paths to death." They are not instances of self-destructiveness, which has been the influential but weak misreading popularized by Norman O. Brown. Rather, they remain dialectical and mythological entities which cannot be reduced to clinical examples. In some sense, the "paths to death" prelude Freud's own Crossing of Identification, his willingness to confront death, his own death. Certainly he wished to die and did die only in his own fashion; he followed his own path to death, but only after two more decades of productive life. The disjunctive gap between Chapters V and VI can be seen better if we omit the last, brief paragraph of V, which was added in 1923. We would pass then directly from a long final paragrah in V that bitterly rejects the notion that there is a drive towards perfection in human beings, to an almost equally long opening paragraph in VI that actually asserts a desire to be wrong about an "opposition between the ego or death instincts and the sexual or life instincts." If the hidden burden at the end of V is Freud's own, rare drive towards perfection of the work, then the equally hidden burden at the start of VI is Freud's anxiety that his own final formulations make any drive towards perfection of the life impossible. But *that* is Freud's Crossing, to choose perfection of the work, and so he moves on in Chapter VI to project or cast out a specious immortality and to introject the sublime Necessity of dying. This makes of VI that final movement I have named by the ratio of *apophrades*, which in rhetoric is the mode of transumption, and in poetry is manifested through images of earliness and lateness. Freud's own belatedness is elegantly shrugged off with the remark, "We have unwittingly steered our course into the harbor of Schopenhauer's philosophy." But Freud's more crucial earliness, his originality which transcends that of any other modern speculator, is masterfully traced in an extraordinary narrative history of the theory of the drives. In this history, as I remarked in Chapter 4, the monistic libido theory of Jung is accurately dismissed as literalistic reductiveness, and Freud's own thoroughgoing dualism is rightly appraised as a figuration that allows him to anticipate future theory, even in the absence of clinical evidence:

> ... I do not dispute the fact that the third step in the theory of the drives, which I have taken here, cannot lay claim to the same degree of certainty as

the two earlier ones—the extension of the concept of sexuality and the hypothesis of narcissism.

As Freud remarks, his own observational evidence for his speculative third step is repetition-compulsion, and there is a prodigious leap from that to the death-drive. But even physiological or chemical language is figurative, as he goes on to remind us; and how then should depth psychology presume to a language other than trope? The brief and beautiful coda that is Chapter VII extends the transumption, and gives us the hidden Freudian metalepsis that I summarized in Chapter 4 in this formula: literal meaning equals anteriority equals an earlier state of meaning equals an earlier state of things equals death. Literal meaning, by a metaleptic leap, is therefore death, while figurative meaning is Eros. Reverse this Freudian formula, and you have part of the context in which the poetic will must operate. Death, time's "it was," is literal meaning; Eros or figuration becomes the will's revenge against time.

How shall we sum up the revisionary pattern of Beyond the Pleasure Principle, its own individual troping of the tradition of crisis-lyric and catastrophe creation? Laplanche eloquently sees the text as granting fantasy an absolute priority, since it mythologizes "a kind of antilife as sexuality, frenetic enjoyment, the negative, repetition-compulsion." But Laplanche need not have been startled, nor should he expect us to be surprised. Rieff long ago pointed out that the idea of the Primal Scene also grants the priority to fantasy, and we can add that primal repression or originary fixation must have a fantasy basis also, since it posits repression before there is anything to be repressed. The peculiar achievement and textual originality of Beyond, among Freud's works, must be found elsewhere.

The originality, still unsettling, remains Freud's initial clinamen or irony in Beyond, which is that the principle of constancy, like the pleasure principle, is transcended by a Schopenhauerian drive to Nirvana. This is Freud's actual "beyonding," as it were, and though it is outrageously speculative, it is not in the fantasy mode of the various primal formulations. Catastrophe is alas not a fantasy, but is the macrocosmic synecdoche of which masochism and sadism form microcosmic parts. It is not self-destruction that energizes the death-drive, but rather the turning of aggression against the self. Freud's astonishing originality is that in Beyond he sees catastrophe as being itself a defense, and I would add that catastrophe creation is thus a defense also. To answer again the question: defense against what? is to return to everything problematic about the poetic will, with its own mutual contaminations of drive and defense.

From a normative Jewish or Christian point of view, catastrophe is allied to the Abyss, and creation is associated with an order imposed upon the Abyss. But from a Gnostic perspective, catastrophe is true creation because it restores the Abyss, while any order that steals its materials from the Abyss is only a sickening to a false creation. Freud's materialistic perspective is obviously neither that of normative theism nor of Gnosis, yet his catastrophe-theories unknowingly border upon Gnosis. For what is the origin of Freud's two final drives, Eros and Thanatos, if it is not catastrophe? Why should there be urges innate in us to restore an earlier condition, unless somehow we had fallen or broken away out of or from that condition? The urges or drives act as our defenses against our belated condition, but these defenses are gains (however equivocal) through change, whereas defenses proper, against the drives, are losses through change, or we might speak of losses that fear further change. Change is the key term, and every cosmic origin of change is seen by Freud as havng been catastrophe.

The origin of defense proper, for Freud, is primal fixation, almost an initial catastrophic origin of drives. Can we account for this very curious speculative principle in Freud, in which there is flight from the drive before the drive has been instituted? The pattern is: defense, followed by catastrophe, followed by drive, or as I would trope this triad: limitation, or contraction, followed by substitution, followed by representation or restitution. I do not for a moment believe that Freud was following, even unconsciously, a Gnostic or Kabbalistic paradigm, but I certainly do believe that he was following, perhaps unconsciously, a similar metaphysical model from Schopenhauer.

Granting that I merely seem to be playing with figurations, permit me to extend the play for a space. What might it mean to say that defense is a movement of limitation or withdrawal, and that the drive is a contrary movement of representation or restitution? Since I have shown defense and drive as contaminating one another anyway, the distinction of contraries here could only be relative. Thus, one could speak of Thanatos as a limiting drive and Eros as a restituting one, but the chiasmic linkage of the two drives (as Laplanche maps it) also brings about a crossing-over of their functions. Again, one could say that reaction-formation, the repetition-compulsions and sublimation are defenses or tropes of limitation, while turning against the self, repression and the negation that mingles projection and introjection are more nearly defenses of restitution. It is suggesive that Thanatos as a drive thus would be more closely allied to reaction-formations, compulsions to repeat, and the "cultural" defense of sublimation, whereas sado-masochism, repression and introjection become the fantasies of Eros, the losses engendered by its drive.

Freud, during a few weeks in July and August of 1938, wrote his unfinished *An Outline of Psychoanalysis*. The little book is difficult and rewarding, and has the peculiar authority of being Freud's last writing of any

length. Perhaps because of the aggressive stance signaled by Freud's Intro-
ductory Note, the dualism of the drives is stated with a singular and positive
harshness. Both drives are called conservative, indeed almost regressive
forces, and deeply contaminate one another, as when Freud bluntly remarks
that "the sexual act is an act of aggression having as its purpose the most
intimate union." The darkness of this final vision of the drives emerges most
clearly when both self-destructiveness or the death-drive and libido or Eros
become outriders on our way to oblivion, allegorical and ironic guides to the
last things:

> Some portion of self-destructiveness remains permanently within, until it at
> length succeeds in doing the individual to death, not, perhaps, until his
> libido has been used up or has become fixated in some disadvantageous
> way. . . .

What begins to be clear is that the drives and the defenses are modeled
upon poetic rhetoric, whether or not one believes that the unconscious
somehow is structured like a language. Eros or libido *is* figurative meaning: the
death-drive *is* literal meaning. The defenses *are* tropes, and thus constitute
the contaminating aspects of both Eros and the death-drive. Eros and Thanatos take the shape of a chiasmus, but this is because the relation between
figurative and literal meaning in language is always a crossing-over.

It is a curious truth that figurative meaning or Eros is "more conspicu-
ous and accessible to study" than literal meaning or the death-drive. If my
analogue holds at all, then sadism and masochism are over-literalizations of
meaning, failures in Eros and so in the possibilities of figurative language. Or
perhaps we might speak of a "regression of libido," a fall into metonymizing,
as being due to a loss of faith in the mind's capacity to accept the burden of
figuration. Sexual "union" is after all nothing but figurative, since the joining
involved is merely a yoking in act and not in essence. The act, in what we
want to call normal sexuality, is a figuration for the unattainable essence.
Sado-masochism, as a furious literalism, denies the figurative representation
of essence by act.

Freud concluded "that the death drives are by their nature mute and
that the clamour of life proceeds for the most part from Eros." Can we
interpret this as meaning that wounded narcissism becomes physical aggression because the loss of self-esteem is also a loss in the language of Eros?
Wounded narcissism is at the origins of poetry also, but in poetry the blow to
self-esteem strengthens the language of Eros, which defends the poetic will
through all the resources of troping. Lacking poetry, the sado-masochist
yields to the literalism of the death-drive precisely out of a rage against literal
meaning. When figuration and sado-masochism are identified, as in Swin-

burne or Robinson Jeffers, then we find always the obsession with poetic *belatedness* risen to a terrible intensity that plays out the poetic will's revenge against time by the unhappy substitution of the body, another's body or one's own, *for* time. Raging against time, forgetting that only Eros or figuration is a true revenge against time, the sado-masochist over-literalizes his revenge and so yields to the death-drive.

In my reading of *Beyond*'s Chapter V as Freud's *askesis*, his own sublimation, I implicitly questioned the coherence of the defense of sublimation even as I centered upon the hidden metaphor of contamination. I return to that metaphor for my conclusion. When drive is viewed as defense, then drive becomes trope or myth, cosmological rhetoric rather than biological instinct. Yet Freud had not waited until 1919, or even until *On Narcissism* in 1915, to reveal this mutual contamination of drive and defense. At least as early as the essay *Taboo and Emotional Ambivalence* in 1912, which was to become the second chapter of *Totem and Taboo*, he had recognized that his fundamental concepts necessarily had contaminated one another by what he called a "mutual inhibition":

> As a result of the repression which has been enforced and which involves a loss of memory—an amnesia—the motives for the prohibition (which is conscious) remain unknown; and all attempts at disposing of it by intellectual processes must fail, since they cannot find any basis of attack. The prohibition owes its strength and its obsessive character precisely to its unconscious opponent, the concealed and undiminished desire—that is to say, to an internal necessity inaccessible to conscious inspection. The ease with which the prohibition can be transferred and extended reflects a process which falls in with the unconscious desire and is greatly facilitated by the psychological conditions that prevail in the unconscious. The instinctual desire is constantly shifting in order to escape from the *impasse* and endeavors to find substitutes—substitute objects and substitute acts—in place of the prohibited ones. In consequence of this, the prohibition itself shifts about as well, and extends to any new aims which the forbidden impulse may adopt. Any fresh advance made by the repressed libido is answered by a fresh sharpening of the prohibition. The mutual inhibition of the two conflicting forces produces a need for discharge, for reducing the prevailing tension; and to this may be attributed the reason for the performance of obsessive acts. . . .

Here the defense of repression and the drive of Eros are so deeply interlocked as to produce taboo, which is the masterpiece of emotional ambivalence, and is the foundation of all literary allegory or irony. Angus Fletcher, in his seminal study of allegory, relates the poetic will's quest to overcome taboo to the trope of transumption, which I have shown to be the ancient rhetorical equivalent of Freud's *Verneinung*, that negation which mingles the defenses of projection and introjection. I shall conclude here by comparing the introjective aspect of the Freudian negation to its parallel in the poet's transumptive will.

Freudian negation and poetic transumption both are instances of psychical duplicity, and both ultimately depend upon a metaphysicial dualism. The Freudian *Verneinung* involves the formulation of a previously repressed feeling, desire or thought, which returns into consciousness only by being affectively disowned, so that defense continues. To carry the truth into the light while still denying it means that one introjects the truth cognitively, while projecting it emotionally. Few insights, even in Freud, are so profound as this vision of negation, for no other theoretical statement at once succeeds as well in tracing the epistemological faculty convincingly to so primitive an origin, or accounts nearly so well for the path by which thought sometimes can be liberated from its sexual past. Since the ego is always a bodily ego, the defenses of swallowing-up and spitting-out, though fantasies, still acknowledge cognitively the ultimate authority of the fact.

I want to contrast to Freud's negation the equivalent process in Vico, for Vico is the great precursor theoretician of the poetic will and of its revisionary ratio that I have called transumption (following Fletcher). What Freud calls the drives, Vico calls "ignorance" or "not understanding the things." Here is Vico on the mingled process of projection and introjection, an ambivalence which for him rises out of the bodily ego, out of a situation in which the ego is ignorant of origins and of the relation between cause and effect:

> . . . man in his ignorance makes himself the rule of the universe, for in the examples cited he has made of himself an entire world. So that, as rational metaphysics teaches that man becomes all things by understanding them, this imaginative metaphysics shows that man becomes all things by *not* understanding them; and perhaps the latter proposition is truer than the former, for when man understands he extends his mind and takes in the things, but when he does not understand he makes the things out of himself and becomes them by transforming himself into them. . . .

Extending the ego to take in the things is not introjection but projection, while the imaginative metaphysics of negation, making "the things out of himself," is a mode of identification, just as introjection is. Not to understand is to suffer drives, and the mind's response is the transformation of defense into a negation that provokes thought. The mutual contamination of drive and defense, of poetic will, with its interplay between literal and figurative, and trope, with its interplay of substitutes, is the common feature linking the speculations of Vico and Freud.

Wallace Stevens, in the closing cantos of his superb crisis-poem *The Auroras of Autumn*, provides me with a coda to my investigation of Freud's own poetic will, which took its revenge against time precisely by contaminating the concepts of defense and of the drive. The trope of transumption, as I have expounded it elsewhere, is the ultimate poetic resource in the will's revenge against time, because transumption undoes the poet's belatedness, the Freudian *Nachträglichkeit*. Stevens, having suffered the anxieites of death-in-life when he first confronted the beautiful menace of the aurora borealis, transumes the northern lights and returns to a vision of earliness, to a Nietzschean and Whitmanian trope of earth's innocence which is *not* a regression, but a true Freudian negation:

> So, then, these lights are not a spell of light,
> A saying out of a cloud, but innocence.
> An innocence of the earth and no false sign
>
> Or symbol of malice. That we partake thereof,
> Lie down like children in this holiness,
> As if, awake, we lay in the quiet of sleep,
>
> As if the innocent mother sang in the dark. . . .

Stevens projects what Freud would have called the Drive of Eros figured by the auroras, its serpentine malice, and simultaneously introjects its literal autumnal aspect, the death-drive, final form of serpentine change. The effect is precisely that of Chapters VI and VII of *Beyond the Pleasure Principle*. A final sublimity is achieved, and though literal death is accepted, the figurative promise of a poetic immortality returns, even as the figurative appears to be cast out. That Freud, more passionately even than the poets, shared in this figurative promise we know from many passages in his works, but never more revealingly than from some belated remarks that he added to an interleaved copy of the 1904 edition of *The Psychopathology of Everyday Life*:

> Rage, anger, and consequently a murderous impulse is the source of superstition in obsessional neurotics: a sadistic component, which is attached to love and is therefore directed against the loved person and repressed precisely because of this link and because of its intensity.—My own superstition has its roots in suppressed ambition (immortality) and in my case takes the place of that anxiety about death which springs from the normal uncertainty of life. . . .

Against the literalism and repetition of the death-drive, Freud sets, so early on, the high figuration of his poetic will to an immortality. Perhaps that may seem some day the truest definition of the Freudian Eros: the will's revenge against time's "it was" is to be carried out by the mind's drive to surpass all earlier achievements. Only the strongest of the poets, and Sigmund Freud, are capable of so luminous a vision of Eros.

Chronology

1856	Born in Freiberg, Moravia (now Přibor, Czechoslovakia), on May 6.
1886	Marries Martha Bernays; begins private medical practice as specialist in nervous diseases.
1894	"The Neuro-Psychoses of Defense."
1895	*Studies on Hysteria* (with Josef Breuer); *Project for a Scientific Psychology* (first published in 1950).
1896	Death of Freud's father, Jakob Freud; first use of the term "psychoanalysis."
1897	Abandons seduction theory; begins self-analysis.
1899	"Screen Memories."
1900	*The Interpretation of Dreams* (published in December 1899 but postdated for the new century).
1902	Appointed Professor Extraordinarius (associate professor) at University of Vienna; meetings of the group that will become the Vienna Psychoanalytic Society.
1905	*Three Essays on the Theory of Sexuality; Jokes and Their Relation to the Unconscious*; Case of Dora ("Fragment of an Analysis of a Case of Hysteria").
1906	Jung makes contact with Freud.
1909	Visits America with Jung and Sandor Ferenczi; receives honorary degree from Clark University and delivers *Five Lectures on Psychoanalysis*.
1910–14	"Wolf Man's" analysis.
1911–15	Papers on psychoanalytic technique.
1913	*Totem and Taboo*; association with Jung terminated.
1914	"On Narcissism"; first mention of the ego ideal, later the superego.
1915	Writes twelve papers on metapsychology, of which only five survive ("Instincts and Their Vicissitudes," "Repression," "The Unconscious," "A Metapsychological Supplement to the Theory of Dreams," "Mourning and Melancholia").
1915–17	Gives *Introductory Lectures* at University of Vienna.
1920	*Beyond the Pleasure Principle*; the death drive postulated.

1921   *Group Psychology and the Analysis of the Ego.*

1923   *The Ego and the Id;* first of thirty-three operations for cancer of the jaw and palate.

1926   *Inhibitions, Symptoms and Anxiety; The Question of Lay Analysis.*

1930   Goethe Prize; *Civilization and Its Discontents;* death of Freud's mother.

1933   Hitler comes to power; burning of Freud's books in Berlin.

1937   "Analysis Terminable and Interminable."

1938   Nazis enter Austria; Freud leaves for England; *An Outline of Psychoanalysis* (published posthumously).

1939   Dies on September 23 in Hampstead, London, at the age of eighty-three.

Contributors

HAROLD BLOOM, Sterling Professor of the Humanities at Yale University, is the author of *The Anxiety of Influence*, *Poetry and Repression* and many other volumes of literary criticism. His forthcoming study, *Freud: Transference and Authority*, attempts a full-scale reading of all of Freud's major writings. He is the general editor of the Chelsea House Library of Literary Criticism.

JACQUES DERRIDA teaches philosophy at the Ecole Normale Supérieure and at Yale University. He is the contemporary French philosopher most influential upon current literary theory in Europe and the United States. His principal books available in English include *Writing and Difference*, *Of Grammatology* and *Dissemination*.

JACQUES LACAN continues to be the major stimulus for the French revision of Freud, which has provided an alternative to the dominant schools of Freudian interpretation, those of Heinz Hartmann and Melanie Klein. Lacan broke with the International Psychoanalytic Association in 1953 and founded the Freudian School of Paris in 1964. His principal books in English are *Ecrits* and *The Four Fundamental Concepts of Psychoanalysis*.

JEAN LAPLANCHE is the principal interpreter of Freud to arise so far out of the school of Lacan. Available in English are his *Life and Death in Psychoanalysis* and (with J.-B. Pontalis) *The Language of Psychoanalysis*.

HERBERT MARCUSE came to the United States as a refugee from Nazi Germany. He taught political philosophy in the United States for many years and became a crucial theorist for the American New Left of the 1960s and 1970s. His legacy is in such books as *Reason and Revolution*, *Negations* and *One-Dimensional Man*.

PAUL RICOEUR, professor of philosophy at the University of Paris (Nanterre, France) and at the University of Chicago, is one of the most eminent contemporary theorists of the art of interpretation. Besides his massive work on Freud, his major books include *The Conflict of Interpretations: Essays in Hermeneutics* and *The Symbolism of Evil*.

PHILIP RIEFF, Benjamin Franklin Professor of Sociology at the University of Pennsylvania, has written on Freud in *The Triumph of the Therapeutic* as well as the pathbreaking *Freud: The Mind of the Moralist*.

LIONEL TRILLING, University Professor at Columbia, was one of the central literary critics of his time. *The Liberal Imagination* remains his best-known book.

JAN HENRIK VAN DEN BERG is a Dutch psychiatrist and historian of psychology. *The Changing Nature of Man* is the best introduction to his original and increasingly influential application of his method to problems of psychiatry. Also available in English are his *A Different Existence* and *Dubious Maternal Love*.

RICHARD WOLLHEIM teaches philosophy at the University of London and at Columbia University. His *Sigmund Freud* is the best brief study available, and should be supplemented by his own *On Art and the Mind*. His other writings include a novel, *A Family Romance*.

Bibliography

Andreas-Salomé, Lou. *The Freud Journal Of Lou Andreas-Salomé*. Translated by Stanley A. Leavy. New York: Basic Books, 1964.

Bersani, Leo. *Baudelaire and Freud*. Berkeley: University of California Press, 1972.

Binswanger, Ludwig. *Being-in-the-World*. Translated by Jacob Needleman. New York: Basic Books, 1963.

Bloom, Harold. *The Breaking of the Vessels*. Chicago: University of Chicago Press, 1982.

Brenner, Charles. *An Elementary Textbook of Psychoanalysis*. New York: Doubleday, 1957.

Brooks, Peter. "Freud's Masterplot: Questions of Narrative." *Yale French Studies* 55/56 (1977): 280–300.

Brown, Norman O. *Life Against Death*. New York: Vintage, 1959.

Burke, Kenneth. "Freud and the Analysis of Poetry." In *The Philosophy of Literary Form*. New York: Vintage, 1957.

Derrida, Jacques. *La Carte Postale de Socrate à Freud et au delà*. Paris: Flammarion, 1980.

———. "Freud and the Scene of Writing." In *Writing and Difference*, translated by Alan Bass. Chicago: University of Chicago Press, 1978.

———. "Fors," translated by Barbara Johnson. *Georgia Review* 31 (Spring 1977): 64–116.

———. "The Purveyor of Truth," translated by Domingo Hulbert et al. *Yale French Studies* 49 (1975): 31–113.

———. "Speculations—on Freud," translated by Ian McLeod. *Oxford Literary Review* 3, no. 2 (1978): 78–97.

Ellenberger, Henri F. *The Discovery of the Unconscious: The History of the Evolution of Dynamic Psychiatry*. New York: Basic Books, 1970.

Fenichel, Otto. *The Psychoanalytic Theory of Neurosis*. New York: W.W. Norton, 1945.

Fiedler, Leslie. "Master of Dreams." *Partisan Review* 34 (1967): 339–56.

Fliess, Robert. *The Psycho-Analytic Reader*. London: Hogarth, 1950.

Freud, Anna. *The Ego and the Mechanisms of Defence*. Translated by Cecil Baines. New York: International Universities Press, 1946.

Freud, Martin. *Sigmund Freud: Man and Father*. New York: Vanguard, 1958.

Freud, Sigmund. *The Complete Psychological Works of Sigmund Freud* (Standard

Edition). Edited by James Strachey. London: Hogarth; New York: W. W. Norton, 1953.

———. *The Freud/Jung Letters*. Translated by Ralph Mannheim and R.F.C. Hull, edited by William McGuire. Princeton: Princeton University Press, 1974.

———. *The Letters of Sigmund Freud: 1873–1939*. Edited by Ernst L. Freud. New York: McGraw-Hill, 1964.

———. *The Letters of Sigmund Freud and Arnold Zweig*. New York: Basic Books, 1970.

———. *The Origins of Psychoanalysis*. Edited by Anna Freud, Marie Bonaparte and Ernst Kris. New York: Basic Books.

———. *A Psychoanalytic Dialogue: The Letters of Sigmund Freud and Karl Abraham*. Edited by Hilda C. Abraham and Ernst L. Freud. New York: Basic Books, 1965.

Hall, Calvin S. *A Primer of Freudian Psychology*. New York: New American Library, 1954.

Hartmann, Heinz; Kris, Ernst; and Loewenstein, Rudolph M. *Papers on Psychoanalytic Psychology*. New York: International Universities Press, 1964.

Hertz, Neil. "Freud and the Sandman." In *Textual Strategies*, edited by Josué V. Harari. Ithaca: Cornell University Press, 1979.

Holland, Norman N. *The Dynamics of Literary Response*. New York: Oxford, 1968.

Hyman, Stanley Edgar. *The Tangled Bank: Darwin, Marx, Frazer, and Freud as Imaginative Writers*. New York: Grosset and Dunlop, 1959.

Jones, Ernest. *The Life and Work of Sigmund Freud*. 3 vols. London: Hogarth, 1956–58.

Kris, Ernst. *The Selected Papers of Ernst Kris*. Edited by Lottie N. Newman. New Haven: Yale University Press, 1975.

Lacan, Jacques. *Ecrits*. Translated by Alan Sheridan. New York: W.W. Norton, 1977.

———. *The Language of the Self*. Translated by Anthony Wilden. Baltimore: Johns Hopkins University Press, 1968.

Laplanche, Jean, and Pontalis, J.-B. *The Language of Psycho-Analysis*. Translated by Donald Nicholson-Smith. London: Hogarth, 1973. ·

Madison, Peter. *Freud's Concept of Repression and Defense*. Minneapolis: University of Minnesota Press, 1961.

Mann, Thomas. "Freud's Position in the History of Modern Thought." In *Past Masters and Other Papers*, translated by H.T. Lowe-Porter. New York: Knopf, 1933.

Mannoni, O. *Freud*. New York: Pantheon, 1971.

Marcuse, Herbert. *One-Dimensional Man*. Boston: Beacon, 1964.

———. *Five Lectures: Psychoanalysis, Politics, and Utopia*. Boston: Beacon, 1970.

Rieff, Philip. *The Triumph of the Therapeutic: Uses of Faith After Freud*. New York: Harper and Row, 1968.

Ruitenbeek, Hendrik M., ed. *Psychoanalysis and Literature*. New York: E.P. Dutton, 1964.

Skura, Meredith Anne. *The Literary Use of the Psychoanalytic Process*. New Haven: Yale University Press, 1981.

Smith, Joseph H., ed. *The Literary Freud: Mechanisms of Defense and the Poetic Will*. Vol. 4, Psychiatry and the Humanities. New Haven: Yale University Press, 1980.

Spector, Jack J. *The Aesthetics of Freud: A Study in Psychoanalysis and Art*. New York: McGraw-Hill, 1972.

Spence, Donald P. *Narrative Truth and Historical Truth*. New York: W.W. Norton, 1982.

Stewart, Walter A. *Psychoanalysis: The First Ten Years, 1888–1898*. New York: Macmillan, 1967.

Sulloway, Frank. *Freud: Biologist of the Mind*. New York: Basic Books, 1979.

Trilling, Lionel. "Freud: Within and Beyond Culture." In *Beyond Culture*. New York: Harcourt, Brace, Jovanovich, 1965.

———. "Freud and Literature." In *The Liberal Imagination*. New York: Viking, 1950.

———. *Mind in the Modern World*. 1972 Jefferson Lectures in the Humanities. New York: Viking, 1972.

Wilden, Anthony. *System and Structure: Essays in Communication and Exchange*. London: Tavistock, 1972.

Wollheim, Richard. *Sigmund Freud*. New York: Viking, 1971.

Wollheim, Richard, and Hopkins, James, eds. *Philosophical Essays on Freud*. Cambridge: At the University Press, 1982.

Acknowledgments

"Eros and Thanatos" by Herbert Marcuse from *Eros and Civilization: A Philosophical Inquiry Into Freud* by Herbert Marcuse, copyright © 1955 by The Beacon Press. Reprinted by permission.

"The Ethic of Honesty" by Philip Rieff from *Freud: The Mind of the Moralist* by Philip Rieff, copyright © 1959, 1961, 1979 by Philip Rieff. Reprinted by permission of University of Chicago Press.

"Neurosis or Sociosis" by J. H. Van Den Berg from *The Changing Nature of Man: Introduction to a Historical Psychology* by J. H. Van Den Berg, copyright © 1961 by W. W. Norton & Co. Reprinted by permission.

"The Deconstruction of the Drive" by Jacques Lacan from *The Four Fundamental Concepts of Psychoanalysis* by Jacques Lacan, copyright © 1978 by W. W. Norton & Co. Reprinted by permission.

"Religion and Fantasy" by Paul Ricoeur from *Freud and Philosophy: An Essay on Interpretation* by Paul Ricoeur, copyright © 1970 by Yale University Press. Reprinted by permission.

"Freud and the Understanding of Art" by Richard Wollheim from *On Art and the Mind: Essays and Lectures* by Richard Wollheim, copyright © 1973 by Richard Wollheim. Reprinted by permission of Allen Lane (Penguin Books).

"The Authentic Unconscious" by Lionel Trilling from *Sincerity and Authenticity* by Lionel Trilling, copyright © 1972 by Harvard University Press. Reprinted by permission.

"The Order of Life and the Genesis of Human Sexuality" by Jean Laplanche, copyright © 1976 by the Johns Hopkins University Press. Reprinted by permission.

"Coming into One's Own" by Jacques Derrida from *Psychoanalysis and The Question of the Text* edited by G. H. Hartman, copyright © 1978 by The English Institute. Reprinted by permission of the Johns Hopkins University Press.

Index